A Final Report
to the People

Volume I

The Bicentennial
of the
United States
of America

A Final Report
to the People

Volume I

The Bicentennial
of the
United States
of America

Prepared and Submitted to the
Congress of the United States
by the
American Revolution
Bicentennial Administration

Library of Congress Catalog Card
Number: 77-71949

American Revolution Bicentennial
Administration · The Bicentennial of the
United States of America:
A Final Report to the People
Washington, D.C.
June 30, 1977
American Revolution Bicentennial
Administration

For sale by the Superintendent of Documents
U.S. Government Printing Office
Washington, D.C. 20402
Stock Number 052-008-00030-1
ISBN 0-9601232-1-0 (Volume I)
ISBN 0-9601232-6-1 (Set)

Preface

"We Did Our Best"

by John W. Warner
Administrator, American
Revolution Bicentennial
Administration

What a great privilege it was to see the Bicentennial in the happy faces of Americans as I visited each of the 50 states and the territories. Their individual achievement is the hallmark of this momentous period in our history.

Untold millions were inspired to do "their own thing" for their community, for their country. Once again, the "can do" spirit—the fiber and strength of this nation throughout its 200 years— molded the Bicentennial into the most massive volunteer movement in peacetime history. These individuals assured America that it got the Bicentennial it wanted, it deserved.

Lasting contributions were made all across our nation. Be they restoration or new construction, educational or cultural programs, or simply the achievement of all the diverse factions of a community having come together to work in harmony for the Bicentennial—they will remain long after the fireworks, the parades and the rhetoric have faded away.

Along with citizen participation came a great learning experience. Americans added to their knowledge of history, particularly of the significance of our blueprints of government in our daily

lives—the Declaration of Independence, the Constitution and the Bill of Rights. We learned how and why those blueprints have enabled this nation, although young in years, to become the oldest continuously surviving democratic republic on earth.

I believe that we now have a better understanding of our past—its greatness as well as its faults—and a better understanding of how all faiths and all nationalities have brought—and continue to bring—something of themselves to American life. We are proud of the richness and the diversity of our many cultures. We are, and always will be, a nation of nations.

The responsibility of the federal government and the state Bicentennial commissions, working together in a totally nonpartisan manner, was to help organize local committees and otherwise encourage citizen participation. We did our best, and our reward is clearly expressed by a short handwritten note I shall always cherish. From a small community came: "Thank you Mr. Government for helping us celebrate in our own way."

To the millions of Bicentennial volunteers—this book is dedicated.

John W. Warner

"An Unqualified Yes"

by Senator Edward W. Brooke
Chairman, American Revolution
Bicentennial Board

As a member of the original American Revolution Bicentennial Commission and Chairman of the ARB Board, I am thoroughly familiar with the difficulties and struggles, the ebb and flow of hopes and plans and the differing viewpoints that faced those charged by Congress with developing the national format for the Bicentennial commemoration. In my judgment, John Warner, ARBA administrator, and his staff fulfilled that congressional mandate in an outstanding and professional manner, to their credit and to the benefit of all Americans. Readers of this report will find ample reason to agree with me.

Measuring the success of the Bicentennial commemoration itself is more difficult since there is no simple

yardstick which applies. Perhaps the best way is to ask the question: "Did the way in which Americans commemorated the nation's 200th birthday contribute to the American dream embodied in the Declaration of Independence, the Constitution and the Bill of Rights?"

Having witnessed, along with all other Americans, the renewed spirit of dedication, patriotism and friendship that flowed across the land on the Bicentennial weekend, it seems to me that the answer is an unqualified yes. Americans used the Bicentennial to renew their faith in themselves, to gain knowledge and understanding of their neighbors, and to begin again the quest for liberty, justice and equality for all.

Edward W. Brooke

"An Overwhelming Experience"

by David L. Wolper
Chairman, American Revolution
Bicentennial Advisory Council

As Chairman of the American Revolution Bicentennial Advisory Council, I have always considered the Council, because of its diversified membership, as representing all the citizens of this country during the Bicentennial. When the Council gathered for its first meeting, there were reports of skepticism throughout the land as to what was going to happen during the Bicentennial year. But, as the Bicentennial year approached, under the brilliant leadership of the Administrator, John W. Warner, and his dedicated staff, and with the strength and support of Senator Edward W. Brooke and the American Revolution Bicentennial Board, and the advice of the Council, the Bicentennial slowly started to take shape.

I can remember telling my friends, early in the year, about the events that were coming up. On occasion I would get a "yawn" and "Oh, yes, that sounds interesting." But, as we got closer to July, the interest grew and grew till on that star-spangled day, July 4, 1976,

our 200th birthday, this great country of ours really experienced what we are all about. We saw, through the various Bicentennial events, that, although we are a patchwork of different cultures, various colors, shapes and sizes, from different regions, when put together we certainly make a beautiful quilt.

Which one of us did not feel the swelling of pride in our country on July 4, 1976? As the day passed, I wondered, "Will this feeling continue? Will we forget this moment?" I think it's important that all of us try to remember the love we had for our country and for each other on that day, and resolve to try to carry that feeling throughout the coming years of our lives.

To all the people in the ARBA, all the Board and Council members, all the advisory groups and state groups that I met with during my years on the Council, I would like to say that it has been an overwhelming experience for me, and I thank all of you for what you contributed and for having had the privilege to share it with you.

Foreword

This five volume report has been prepared for the Congress and the American people as required by Public Law 93-179.

With the filing of this report, the American Revolution Bicentennial Administration (ARBA) is terminated.

The five volumes contain the following information:

—Volume I (this volume): a narrative account from nine perspectives, with color photographs, of America's Bicentennial celebration as it occurred.

—Volume II: an appendix to Volume I which provides detailed lists and brief descriptions of officially endorsed projects; names of persons who served with various national, state and local Bicentennial groups; ARBA staff members; all the officially recognized Bicentennial Communities; tables detailing grant monies; details of federal agency participation; private sector involvement; lists of public information materials produced; and other such information. It includes a limited number of black and white photographs.

—Volumes III, IV and V: a 56 section listing of Bicentennial activities in all the states, territories, the District of Columbia, the Commonwealth of Puerto Rico and foreign countries.

The sections are arranged alphabetically, and each begins with a brief descriptive overview. Following this, the projects and events are listed by city. These activity summaries are based on information reported to the ARBA and contained in the automated Bicentennial Information Network (BINET) system.

These five volumes contain only those events and projects which were reported to, or otherwise came to the attention of, the ARBC or the ARBA. There were undoubtedly thousands more.

Jean McKee

ARBA Acting Administrator

Introduction

The Congressional Mandates

AMERICAN REVOLUTION
BICENTENNIAL COMMISSION
1966–74
Public Law 89–491, 89th Congress

". . . to plan, encourage, develop, and coordinate the commemoration of the American Revolution Bicentennial."

AMERICAN REVOLUTION
BICENTENNIAL ADMINISTRATION
1974–77
Public Law 93–179, 93rd Congress

". . . to coordinate, to facilitate, and to aid in the scheduling of events, activities, and projects of local, State, National, and international significance sponsored by both governmental and nongovernmental entities in commemoration of the American Revolution Bicentennial."

The Themes

Underlying most of the Bicentennial planning and participation was a reaffirmation of our blueprints of government—the Declaration of Independence, the Constitution and the Bill of Rights—the blueprints which enable us to celebrate proudly the 200th anniversary of the oldest continuously surviving democratic republic in the world.

Congress endorsed three themes to give focus to the rich diversity of commemorative activities.

Through *Heritage '76,* we sought to remember our form of government, our Founding Fathers, our forgotten people, the places and things of our past, the events of our past and, most important, our freedoms.

Through *Festival USA,* we celebrated the richness of our diversity, the vitality of our culture, our hospitality, the American scene and the traditions of our people.

Through *Horizons '76,* we planned to shape a better tomorrow by beginning with individual initiative, by drawing inspiration from the innovations of today, by seeking the blessing of liberty for ourselves and others and by setting our Century III goals.

The National Bicentennial Symbol

The American Revolution Bicentennial symbol is derived from the stars, stripes and colors of our nation's flag.

The symbol takes the form of a five-pointed star in white, surrounded by continuous red, white and blue stripes which form a second star. This double star is symbolic of the two centuries which have passed since the American Revolution.

These colorful stripes also evoke a feeling of festivity and suggest the bunting traditionally used in times of celebration throughout the nation.

The symbol is contemporary in design in keeping with the forward-looking goals of the Bicentennial celebration: "To forge a new national commitment, *a new spirit for '76,* a spirit which vitalizes the ideals for which the Revolution was fought; a spirit which will unite the nation in purpose and in dedication to the advancement of human welfare as it moves into its third century."

Contents

The Bicentennial
Approaches

Getting Ready—
The Mood of the Country

2   The republic still lives, Mr. Ben Franklin.

You once challenged your landlady when she asked if you Founding Fathers had produced a republic or a monarchy. "A Republic, Madam, if you can keep it," was your reply.

We have arrived at the 200th anniversary of our nation. We kept faith in freedom. We were diligent in preserving our form of government. We had hope for our future.

The republic endures.

From generation to generation, it has become more challenging to hold together as diverse a society as the United States of America. However, those three great documents—the Declaration of Independence, the Constitution and the Bill of Rights—sustain us in our experiment of government with the consent of the governed. Government of the people, by the people and for the people requires unremitting vigilance and a capacity to deal constantly with new times and new problems.

As Thomas Jefferson observed after 40 years of experience in government: ". . . laws and institutions must go hand in hand with the progress of the human mind. As that becomes more developed, more enlightened, as new discoveries are made, new truths disclosed, and manners and opinions change with the change of circumstances, institutions must advance also, and keep pace with the times."

(preceding pages) Sunrise, Washington, D.C.

(below) Armand-Dumaresque's The Signing of the Declaration of Independence

(opposite page) The Declaration of Independence in the National Archives Rotunda, Washington, D.C.

4

Tension Everywhere

We entered the Bicentennial year having survived some of the bitterest times in our brief history. We cried out for something to draw us together again.

The unsettled period most likely began in 1963 with the assassination of our young President, John F. Kennedy. Many had been uplifted by his leadership and vitality. That emotional euphoria was crushed out.

By 1965, America was heavily involved in an unpopular conflict in Vietnam, where our final troop commitment reached 500,000 and where 50,000 of those Americans died. The war divided our country and caused riots in our homeland.

A weary and disheartened President Lyndon B. Johnson decided in 1968 not to seek office again.

The world reeled in shock at the assassination of Black leader Dr. Martin Luther King, Jr. Shock turned to disbelief when Robert F. Kennedy, brother of the late President, was shot down while campaigning for his party's nomination to the Presidency.

Dr. Martin Luther King, Jr.

President John F. Kennedy gravesite, Arlington National Cemetery, Washington, D.C.

(opposite page) An unsettled period in our history

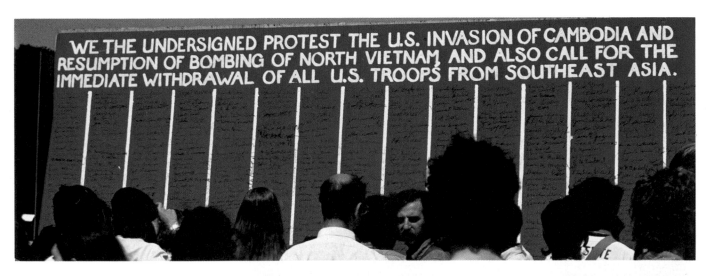

WE THE UNDERSIGNED PROTEST THE U.S. INVASION OF CAMBODIA AND RESUMPTION OF BOMBING OF NORTH VIETNAM AND ALSO CALL FOR THE IMMEDIATE WITHDRAWAL OF ALL U.S. TROOPS FROM SOUTHEAST ASIA.

VIETNAM VETERANS AGAINST THE WAR

LEAVE THE FEAR OF RED TO HORNED BEASTS

From Depths to Pinnacles

Our national spirits were raised to the moon when Astronauts Neil A. Armstrong and Edwin E. Aldrin, Jr. reached that distant body July 20, 1969—only to be dashed to earth less than a year later with the four students killed at Kent State University by a detachment of the Ohio National Guard.

Richard Milhous Nixon was reelected President in 1972 by an overwhelming majority. We were heartened and made proud as the world watched his successes in Peking and Moscow. Our men finally came home from Vietnam (some say we lost that war).

Just as we breathed a halting sigh of relief, a charge of misconduct forced Vice President Spiro T. Agnew to resign.

And Then Watergate

And then came Watergate—the long, demoralizing investigation of President Nixon and his aides for illegal campaign activities, and the subsequent cover-up of those actions.

Through the eyes of television millions of Americans saw Congress debating impeachment. President Nixon resigned before the proceedings were completed.

Gerald R. Ford was the first President who was not elected either Vice President or President. Our new leader asked Americans to "confirm me with your prayers."

After a decade of racial tensions, assassinations, scandal, rising inflation, embattled campuses and eroding public trust, what was there left to celebrate?

There was plenty.

(opposite page) Astronaut Edwin E. Aldrin, Jr. on the moon, as photographed by Astronaut Neil A. Armstrong

7

8

America Kept Faith

America had kept faith with its people and its people had kept faith with America.

All of these events had not proven our system to be faulty. They had proven that our system works like no other. They had shown the strength of those three great documents. They had proved our Founding Fathers to be brilliant architects.

George Washington summed up the soul of America in his first inaugural address: ". . . the preservation of the sacred fire of liberty and the destiny of the republican model of government are justly considered, perhaps, as *deeply*, as *finally*, staked on the experiment entrusted to the hands of the American people."

(clockwise, beginning upper left) Statue of Liberty, New York City; Washington Monument, Washington, D.C.; Cathedral Group, Grand Teton National Park, Wyoming; Gannett Peak on Wind River, Wyoming; Table Rock Formation, Navajo Reservation, Arizona; Jefferson Memorial, Washington, D.C.; The White House, Washington, D.C.

Still an Experiment

A noted historian in our own time, Arthur M. Schlesinger, Jr., echoed Washington's theme: "Two centuries later it is still an experiment and still in the hands of the American people. Each generation must prove anew its devotion to the adventure of self–government."

As we looked toward July 4, 1976, we found reassurance in our three great documents—resurgence of belief in ourselves.

The Bicentennial planners might have settled for a world's fair such as the Centennial exhibition in Philadelphia. But this was another day, a different time. The planners wisely chose another course.

Bring Everybody Together

The Bicentennial was to become a hometown affair. The most important Bicentennial undertakings would bring dissidents as well as neighbors and friends together in common purpose.

So, too, Americans saw their Bicentennial not only as a commemoration of what had gone before, but as an opportunity to commit themselves to the problems and concerns of what would come in the days ahead.

So, Mr. Franklin, the things we learned about ourselves as we came through those troubled years just prior to our Bicentennial set the stage for our celebration.

The principles embodied in our founding documents had once again survived the test—proven and stronger. We were ready to celebrate our strengths—not our weaknesses. We were ready to celebrate as only Americans can.

And celebrate we did ! ! !

Americans everywhere were ready to celebrate

The national Bicentennial flag

9

The Fourth of July
Weekend

The Bicentennial Peaks—
July 2, 3, 4, 5, 1976

12

O beautiful for spacious skies
For amber waves of grain,

For purple mountain majesties
Above the fruited plain!

America! America!
God shed His grace on thee

And crown thy good with brotherhood
From sea to shining sea!

From sea to shining sea—we celebrated. Voices lifting unashamedly in song, tears welling as the flag went by. With good will and cheer, with prayer, picnics and parades, with joy and with solemnity—we celebrated. Above all, we celebrated with pride in our past and confidence in our future.

Bicentennial weekend, July 1976, literally burst across the nation, awesome in its variety, decked out in the splendor of tall sailing ships and musical extravaganzas, touched with the dignity of formal readings of the historic document which gave birth to the nation—the Declaration of Independence.

Across mountains and valleys, along seacoasts and rivers, on prairies and plains and on far-flung islands, America welcomed its third century so as to reflect the greatness of the nation, its spirit and strength. It was a celebration of, by and for the people.

(preceding pages) Operation Sail '76—
New York Harbor, July 4

Nation Steady on Course

To the world, and to Americans themselves, the Bicentennial weekend showed the face of a nation that had pulled itself together after turbulent and difficult times, a nation steadied on course as it sailed into its third century.

When the weekend was over, Americans went back to their everyday pursuits, at work, in schools, at home and at play, reassured that the grand experiment in self-government still glowed as a beacon of liberty. They were filled with renewed determination that the beacon would shine brightly for future generations.

OPSAIL '76 host ship, the U.S. Coast Guard bark Eagle, *New York Harbor*

Colonial fifers and drummers at Independence Hall, Philadelphia

On the town green, Colonial Williamsburg, Virginia

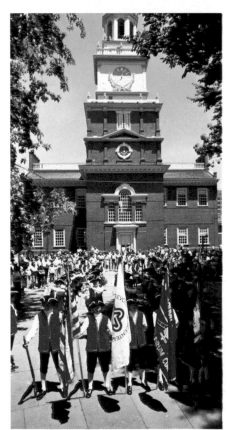

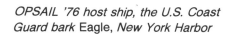

14   The Focus Within the Bicentennial

Just as the signing of the Declaration of Independence on July 4, 1776 was neither the beginning nor the end of the Revolution, the celebration of that event 200 years later was neither the start nor the finish of the Bicentennial commemoration. The weekend of July 2 through 5 did, however, give focus to the commemoration and did accentuate the depth and excitement of the entire Bicentennial, as planned and produced in every nook and cranny of the country in ways as diverse as the people themselves.

And on Sunday, July 4th, Bicentennial day, television provided the nation with a great exposition that some felt would be missing during the historic period—an exposition of the nation itself.

It might be useful to recall that Viking I was circling the planet Mars in search of a landing site as the nation exploded in celebration. One hundred years before, a brash, young country boasted of its technological accomplishments with the Centennial International Exhibition in Philadelphia. In 1976, Viking's venturesome trip into outer space was testimony enough to the nation's technology. In 1976, America turned inward to find itself and renew its spirit.

Another historical footnote. Just one hundred years ago our Western frontier was still open. While the world participated in the Centennial exhibition in Philadelphia, General George A. Custer and his troops were wiped out by Indians led by Sitting Bull at the Battle of the Little Big Horn.

*Artist's concept of Viking
mission to Mars*

The Weekend Unfolds

Trying to recapture the drama, flavor and emotions of the Bicentennial weekend in words is like trying to describe an autumn sunset in New England, the first snow of winter in the Rockies, or waves crashing against the rocks on California's Monterey coastline. Beautiful, radiant, glowing, sparkling, awesome, many-hued, peaceful—descriptive words abound, but the impact and meaning of that epochal interlude rest with each individual, in the eye of the beholder.

A look back at the activities can only hint at the magnitude and flavor of America's 200th birthday salute. Those who shared in it will cherish the memory; others must rely on historical appraisals which will follow.

One thing is certain—Americans followed John Adams' dictum in a letter to his wife, Abigail, just after the Founding Fathers approved the Declaration: "It ought to be commemorated as the day of deliverance, by solemn acts of devotion to God Almighty. It ought to be solemnized with pomp and parade, with shows, games, sports, guns, bells, bonfires, and illuminations, from one end of this continent to the other, from this time forward, forever more."

The Archives, decorated for the celebration

The Bicentennial Weekend

Fittingly, the Bicentennial weekend opened on Friday evening, July 2, with solemn ceremonies at the National Archives in Washington, D.C. honoring the Declaration of Independence and the other two blueprints of democracy—the Constitution and the Bill of Rights. President Gerald R. Ford, Speaker of the House Carl A. Albert and Chief Justice of the United States Warren E. Burger led the nation in homage to the founding documents and set a reflective tone for the weekend celebration. Their appearance together—heads of the three branches of government—symbolized the checks and balances and unity inherent in the government of the United States.

The precious documents were then displayed as part of a special 76 hour public vigil, during which time over 25,000 visitors signed the official register, their names to be placed in a national time capsule and opened during the Tricentennial.

76 hour vigil begins at National Archives

For the next three days, the people threw what TV commentator Walter Cronkite described as "the greatest, most colossal birthday party in 200 years." The automated Bicentennial Information Network, developed by the American Revolution Bicentennial Commission (ARBC) and afterward maintained by the American Revolution Bicentennial Administration (ARBA), catalogued nearly 4,000 events for the weekend. Thousands of other activities, though not officially registered, were also part of the fabric of the weekend.

Signing first page of book for time capsule

Parades, Parades, Parades

With the possible exception of Mom's apple pie, nothing is so "American" as parades, and they were central to the birthday festivities. Although it rained on a few of them, most were sun-kissed and tagged as the "grandest" ever held with the "biggest" gathering of cheering spectators.

The granddaddy of them all was the six hour long *Parade of States* in Philadelphia on Sunday afternoon, which drew two million onlookers. All 50 states were represented among the 200 groups parading in the city where independence was first declared.

Bands parade along Main Street, U.S.A.

20

In the nation's capital, 500,000 people jammed Constitution Avenue on Saturday morning at 11:00 a.m. for a mammoth parade led by Vice President and Mrs. Nelson A. Rockefeller and the Grand Marshal, country and western singer Johnny Cash. The flavor of America as a nation of nations came from Scottish pipers and Irish dancers, Czechs and Slovaks in European costume, Dutch "Klompen Dancers" in wooden shoes, a German band, Koreans in stovepipe hats and Chinese jostling a dragon. There were Bolivians, Greeks, Italians, Filipinos and Serbs. The Navajo code-talkers, an elite group of former U.S. Marines who used their Indian language in World War II as a unique radio code to confuse enemy listeners, drew appreciative applause.

Elsewhere during the glorious weekend. . . . Mobile, Alabama, parade watchers had grandstand seats as floats depicting the spirit of America moved through Ladd Memorial Stadium. Wayne, New Jersey celebrated with a parade retracing the route of the Continental Army in 1780. And in the Virgin Islands, the parade lasted three days: July 3 on the island of St. Croix, July 4 on St. John and July 5 on St. Thomas.

(top) Vice President and Mrs. Rockefeller, honorary co-chairpersons of the Happy Birthday, USA! July 4th weekend events in the nation's capital, wave to crowd

(left) People line Constitution Avenue in front of Smithsonian Museum of Arts and Industry

(opposite page) Spectators and participants

The *Peoria Journal-Star,* editorializing on a local parade, put all the parades into perspective: "A woman holding a small child was watching the city's parade and she remarked, 'It makes you want to believe in the country.' That, of course, is the whole idea and one suspects thousands, moved to remember our hard beginnings, our earnest struggles, our triumphs and tragedies, and the great distance we have come in so relatively short a time, share her sentiments."

Picnics, Festivals, Fairs

There were picnics, festivals and fairs everywhere during the holiday weekend. Clinton, Missouri typified the "something for everybody" tradition.

A midday dinner of barbecued chicken was followed by the dedication of the Henry County Museum and Cultural Center. The afternoon was crammed with gospel singing, country and western music, beard-growing and male beauty contests, watermelon eating and seed-spitting battles.

Maynard Knutson gave his locally famous rendition of the *Battle Hymn of the Republic* on a saw. An egg-throwing contest, mainly for youngsters, drew several adults. None could top the winning strategy of eleven year olds Sarabeth Hendrich and Sherrill Dulaban. Their secret? According to a smiling Sarabeth, standing triumphantly in the egg-spattered street, "Just throw it very softly," she said, emphasizing the word "very."

Bicentennial balloons along parade route

Outdoor Bicentennial activities—crafts, biking, log-rolling, music

Two women, Mrs. Sandra Lindsay and Mrs. Dinah Scott, won free movie passes by defeating three men in a nail-driving contest, after which the firing of Larry Shank's Civil War cannon got the frog jumping and turtle races underway.

Like most celebrations across the nation, Clinton's was a home-grown event for hometown people. Jerry Osborn, master of ceremonies, claimed he could recognize 90 percent of the faces in the crowd. "We've been trying to promote the idea that you can stay in Clinton, and you don't really have to go anywhere else."

On the 4th of July, 1976, most of the residents of Henry County didn't go anywhere else. They stayed home. They celebrated with friends and neighbors. This was the spirit of the Bicentennial throughout the nation.

24

An active America kept the 4th of July in motion—in each of the 12,566 Bicentennial Communities

Here, There, Everywhere

26

Folks in Durham, North Carolina staged a distinctively Dixie bash, complete with barbecued pork and plenty of chitterlings and bean pie.

In Bartow, Florida, America's oldest citizen, Charlie Smith, celebrated two birthdays—the nation's 200th and his own 134th. Because he can't recall his exact birthdate, Mr. Smith traditionally has marked it on July 4th, which is the anniversary of his sale at a slave auction in 1854. He calls himself "a United States Man."

For people in San Francisco, it was a double-barreled Bicentennial that also commemorated the anniversary of the arrival of the first Spanish settlers only days before the Declaration of Independence was signed in Philadelphia.

San Antonio, Texas recalled its Spanish origins, as well as its German settlers and its frontier beginnings, with a festive weekend of arts and crafts fairs, canoe races, square dances and band concerts.

New Yorkers celebrated their own unique mix of people and cultures. Throughout lower Manhattan, Turks danced, Armenians served shish kebab, the Irish sang folk songs. Throngs of New Yorkers enjoyed events representing the Urals and the Mediterranean, Northern Europe and Asia. There were Greek, Ukrainian, Slovak and Korean events, as well as Polish, Hungarian and Lithuanian. The Italian festival was a kaleidoscope of food, games and flea markets.

In New Orleans, a city that never needs an excuse to throw a party, the air vibrated with traditional Dixieland jazz, a persuasive testimonial to the influence of Black Americans on the nation's musical heritage. The city dedicated a square to Louis Armstrong, King of Jazz, and also paid tribute to its French-Spanish-Creole-Cajun ancestry with a variety of culinary, art and film festivals.

Hartford, Connecticut and Denver, Colorado dedicated statues honoring the Revolutionary General, Casimir Pulaski, of Poland. Dallas, Texas unveiled a larger-than-life-size bronze statue of Dr. Martin Luther King, Jr.

There was a state fair of mountain arts and crafts in Ripley, West Virginia. Delegate Caesar Rodney's dash—despite his illness—from Dover, Delaware to Philadelphia in 1776 to break a tie and ensure the vote for independence was reenacted. Honolulu held a Polynesian arts, crafts and music festival. A Pony Express ride was made from Las Cruces, New Mexico to El Paso, Texas. A barbecue paralleling one held in 1876 was arranged in Newport, Arkansas, and a July 4, 1876 play was restaged in Virginia City, Nevada.

Marlon Morris, a 14 year old Maywood, Illinois youth, recopied the entire Declaration of Independence because he thought the originial was too dim. *Bikecentennial '76* riders along the transcontinental trail celebrated wherever they happened to be.

American Samoa throbbed with a three day fiesta featuring copra-cutting, spear-chucking and interisland canoe racing. Guam had a naval review, beginning at one minute past midnight, to herald the 4th. The All-Alaska Logrolling Championship was held in Sitka.

There was an auto race up Pikes Peak, a vintage airshow in Colorado Springs, Colorado and a buffalo chip-throwing contest in Salida, Colorado. New Philadelphia, Ohio had a hog-calling contest, and Cairo, Georgia recreated the Grady County marble games of 1876. There was an antique tractor pull in Calamus, Iowa, and hot air balloons went up over Seward, Nebraska. The all-Indian rodeo finals were held in Flagstaff, Arizona.

And it went on and on.

America's faces . . . reveal our many roots

28　Birthday Cakes

No birthday party is complete without cake, and America's 200th was no exception. There were cakes of all kinds, shapes and sizes.

Philadelphia, with the assistance of the Kitchens of Sara Lee and a French cook with the unlikely name of Bernardo, concocted a five story high chocolate masterpiece weighing 49,000 pounds. The red, white and blue cake was decorated with the seals of all the states and territories, as well as 120 historical scenes, and was topped by an American eagle. After the party, the cake was cut up and donated to charitable institutions.

Baltimore came up with a 50 by 20 by 8 foot plywood dummy cake in the shape of the continental United States. It contained frosted, prewrapped slices of pound cake in souvenir Bicentennial boxes. The slices were sold, at $2.25 each, to finance historic restoration projects in Baltimore. The cake was floated by barge to the site of the dusk-to-dawn extravaganza at Fort McHenry. It was there, while the flag flew proudly through a British attack during the War of 1812, that Francis Scott Key was inspired to write the moving words which later became our national anthem.

A birthday cake was served at the National Archives on July 4th, with the U.S. Army Band playing *Happy Birthday*. Slices were given to visitors filing through the Rotunda to view the documents of democracy during the special 76 hour vigil.

In Champaign, Illinois, the entire population was invited to bring their own cake to festivities and share it with family and friends.

Multi-layer birthday cakes at Philadelphia (bottom left), Washington, D.C. (bottom right), San Francisco (opposite page, bottom right) . . . and homemade cakes in backyards throughout the land

Something Personal, Special

By design, the Bicentennial commemoration spanned several years, with activities and events occurring well before and well after the Bicentennial weekend. However, there is no doubt that Americans considered July 4, 1976 to be something personal and special, apart even from the rest of the weekend. That was the day, 200 years ago, that our nation began. It was now the day when our third century was beginning.

Each American will have a private memory of the day, but television provided the broadest picture and its own memorable record. Glimpses of what television saw and presented to the nation that day can best describe it.

Sunday morning, July 4, begins with live TV coverage at Independence Hall, Philadelphia; Fort McHenry, Baltimore; and Old Faithful in Yellowstone National Park, Wyoming

TV from Dawn's Early Light

The TV networks began coverage early in the morning and continued through the day and into the night.

Early Sunday risers or late Saturday bed-goers, watching the special telecast on Metromedia stations, must have tingled to see the flag still flying proudly over Fort McHenry as the strains of *The Star-Spangled Banner* poured forth.

Millions of Americans started the Sunday off by attending religious services. TV zoomed in on several of these services, including the major interdenominational program, *A Nation under God—The Birth and Rebirth of Freedom,* at Independence Hall in Philadelphia.

As many of their print brethren editorialized later, TV did a bang-up job. To quote just one, *The Tulsa (Oklahoma) Daily World:* "Give television credit for bringing them [July 4th activities] into our homes—live and in color. It gave us a sense of drama and sweep, of the American Oneness out of diversity, and the remembrance of where we have been and what we have done."

TV people put a lot of time and effort into getting ready to cover the day's events, and no one was disappointed. The ARBA contributed to the effort through its Bicentennial Weekend Media Information Center, set up to assist the nation's media in covering the big party.

The Information Center staff, located in a Jackson Place townhouse near the White House, had worked for several months researching interesting and major activities scheduled to take place over the weekend and established what the military might call an "Operations Control Center" to provide minute by minute updating of events as they happened.

32

Parade of Tall Ships

The most spectacular, awe-inspiring panorama of the day had to be the parade of 16 majestic tall ships from 14 countries, sailing into New York Harbor and up the Hudson. They dramatically recalled the nation's maritime history and highlighted international participation in the Bicentennial.

An estimated six million people lining the shores, some 20,000 small boats churning about, the boom of welcoming cannon—who will forget that scene?

As the stately vessels moved slowly past the Statue of Liberty with her invitation to the world to "Give me your tired, your poor,/Your huddled masses yearning to breathe free, . . ."—who viewing that scene, in person or on television, did not remember the waves of immigrants pouring onto these shores and, once here, building a nation?

In an electronic hop, skip and jump around the country, television covered the big and the small, catching faces and feelings, the simple and the dramatic . . .

—The moving reading of the Declaration of Independence at Independence Hall by Marian Anderson, the famous contralto; a Kiowa powwow in Carnegie, Oklahoma; a buffalo stampede and rodeo in Greeley, Colorado; a husband-calling contest in Polk County, Iowa; and wingwalking, riverboat races and musical variety in St. Louis, Missouri.

TV shows spectators viewing OPSAIL '76 in New York

The cameras also focus on Sunday morning church services in a mission in America's southwest, in the Old North Church, Boston and in Lancaster, Pennsylvania

—Conestoga wagons and prairie schooners trundling into Valley Forge, Pennsylvania, ending an almost two year odyssey across all 48 continental states, recreating in reverse the nation's westward expansion. They brought with them over 22 million signatures on dedication scrolls gathered along the way, the names hopefully to be microfilmed and placed in a time capsule as a testimony of faith.

The President spoke at the encampment early Sunday morning, recalling the sacrifices of the Continental Army at Valley Forge and commending "The sturdy wagon trains that have returned here, the wonderful people who drove them and those along the way who rededicate themselves to the great principles of the Declaration of Independence, [who] offer heartwarming proof that our American adventure has just begun."

—Bells tolling across the nation, timed to the peal of the Independence Hall Tower Bell at exactly 2:00 p.m. EDT, ringing for two minutes, one for each century. The President ringing the ship's bell on the deck of the aircraft carrier, *U.S.S. Forrestal,* in New York Harbor, one stroke for each of the original 13 states.

—The realistic recreation of Confederate General George E. Pickett's charge during the Battle of Gettysburg, which raged July 1, 2 and 3, 1863. His defeat was a turning point of the Civil War. The site brought to mind Lincoln's words when the nation was only 87 years old: "It is for us, the living, rather to be dedicated here to the unfinished work which they who fought here have thus far so nobly advanced. It is rather for us to be here dedicated to the great task remaining before us—that this nation, under God, shall have a new

birth of freedom; and that government of the people, by the people, for the people, shall not perish from the earth." Still appropriate now, during the Bicentennial.

—The Mormon Tabernacle Choir and its beautiful televised rendition of the *Battle Hymn of the Republic,* the Boston Pops playing the *1812 Overture* under the baton of its ebullient conductor, Arthur Fiedler, and the joyous crowd of 400,000 in Boston gathering to listen and enjoy.

—And fireworks . . . bathing the Statue of Liberty in fiery colors, illuminating the Washington Monument, punctuating the Boston Pops performance.

Memories, some fading, some still vivid—creations of the American people, documented by television. July 4, 1976, America, 200 years later. We loved it.

Putting Down New Roots

34

Other events of the weekend brought lasting value to the Bicentennial. Trees were planted, parks dedicated, ground broken, historic buildings renovated and reopened, many with new purposes. Americans expressing their belief in the future in a concrete way.

And on Monday

On Monday, July 5, President Ford welcomed new citizens during naturalization ceremonies at Monticello, Thomas Jefferson's Virginia home. The President summed it all up: "After two centuries, there is still something wonderful about being an American. If we cannot quite express it, we know what it is. You know what it is or you would not be here today. Why not just call it patriotism?"

Bicentennial weekend not only had a lot to say about the state of the nation. It also had much to say about the state of the Bicentennial, which was basically a neighborhood effort, without a "world's fair" centerpiece. Its true nature and magnitude had been difficult for many to grasp. The Bicentennial weekend brought it forcefully home.

Naturalization ceremony at Monticello

The Weekend Didn't "Just Happen"

Even the most casual observer had to have realized the time and effort, dedication and sacrifice that had gone into making the Bicentennial weekend a reality. Though the weekend events and activities represented only about five percent of the total effort to commemorate the Bicentennial, they brought the whole massive enterprise into focus.

Parades, pageants, ceremonies, all took preparation and planning. ARBA Administrator John W. Warner called the Bicentennial the greatest volunteer effort in the history of peacetime America. Bicentennial weekend proved it.

Over a million people crowd monument grounds in Washington, D.C.

(opposite page) Marching units of all types show colors

OPSAIL '76

The smash hit of the weekend, the parade of tall ships, well illustrates the stirring nature of the Bicentennial.

As *The New York Daily News* put it: ". . . recognition is due the man who conceived Operation Sail, Frank Braynard, a founder of [New York City's] South Street Seaport Museum.

"Braynard did far more than spawn the idea. He devoted five years to making it a reality, and it was thanks to his perseverance that the tall-masted ships sailed from all corners of the globe to take part in New York's pageant."

Along the way, Braynard's idea grew to embrace world-wide sailing organizations, city, state and federal government agencies, and foreign governments. It attracted funds from a variety of sources, including a timely seed grant from the ARBC. Like a magnet, it drew into New York Harbor the largest gathering of sailing ships in peacetime history.

It also drew the *International Naval Review*, an impressive assemblage of military vessels from many nations. They formed a backdrop for the parade of tall ships up the Hudson.

On July 4, 224 sailing ships, which represented 30 countries and included most of the world's tall ships, enthralled the world.

New York wasn't the finish. The ships then scattered to host cities up and down the Atlantic coast and along the Great Lakes via the St. Lawrence Seaway. In every community, crowds jammed aboard, savoring the last remaining symbols of an historic era.

44 Wagon Train

The *Bicentennial Wagon Train Pilgrimage to Pennsylvania* was another example. Sponsored by the Pennsylvania Bicentennial Commission, the eastward trek of wagons and horses touched hundreds of communities, included thousands of riders and involved every state's Bicentennial commission in planning and execution. Wagon Train also received assistance from the Gulf Oil Corporation, as well as grant funds from the ARBA, which was carrying out its congressional mandate to stimulate and encourage events of national significance.

Bicentennial Wagon Train Pilgrimage to Pennsylvania *celebrates at Valley Forge*

46   **Why the Bells Tolled**

The simultaneous ringing of bells across the nation on July 4th at 2:00 p.m. EDT illustrates the coordinating role played by the ARBA.

The 25 member ARB Advisory Council had requested that the ARBA staff explore ways and means to encourage unifying themes for the Bicentennial weekend to help Americans join together in the celebration.

The administrator learned that communities across the country were independently planning flag tributes, prayer services, readings of the Declaration of Independence, bell-ringing, candle-lighting and other activities which, if coordinated, could provide nationwide expressions of unity and focal points for the 200th birthday celebration.

Bell-ringing was singled out as the one activity that could best happen everywhere at the same time and was suggested by the ARBA in news releases and letters to Bicentennial communities. The suggestion caught hold. The bells tolled across the country to mark the 200th anniversary of the nation's birth.

At 2:00 p.m. EDT President Ford rings bell aboard U.S.S. Forrestal, *as bells peal simultaneously throughout America*

It Was a Peaceful Weekend

Something that did not happen provides a measure of the milestone reached by the United States as it entered its third century.

There was no violence. This perhaps was the most astounding feature of the weekend, considering the turmoil of the years preceding the celebration. Assassinations, protests, bombings—all had become part of the American scene during the dark days of the sixties and early seventies. There were fears the birthday party could be marred by violence.

But the weekend went off with hardly a murmur of dissent and no reported terrorism. In fact, several major cities noted a decrease in criminal activity as people joined together in celebration.

Washington, D.C., usually a focus of dissent and often the scene of major confrontations, was typical. On the night of the 4th, over a million people gathered on the Mall for the *National Pageant of Freedom and Fireworks Display.* While hoping for the best, officials were prepared for the worst.

What they got was the most peaceful mass gathering anybody could remember. They also got the area's biggest traffic jam and bus snarl, but even then the crowd was peaceable and good-humored.

Washington did have its protest demonstrations over the weekend, but they succeeded only in emphasizing the inherent right of Americans to disagree, the very fundamental that was being celebrated.

The American Nationalist Socialist White People's Party drew a few curious onlookers at its rally mid-Saturday afternoon in Lafayette Park, across from the White House, and this comment from one observer: "It's amazing how silly they sound, but it's their right."

The People's Bicentennial Commission, a group formed to "provide an alternate way to commemorate the Bicentennial," expected 200,000 protestors against big business but only attracted an estimated 5,000 to the Mall on the 4th of July. Despite the thousands gathering for the fireworks display, there were no confrontations or untoward incidents.

And that's the way it was across the nation.

48

Fireworks . . . (opposite page) Statue of Liberty, New York City; (this page, clockwise, beginning upper right) John F. Kennedy Center for the Performing Arts, Washington, D.C.; Jefferson Memorial Arch, St. Louis; Charles River Esplanade, Boston

50

Pundits Were Pleased

The nation's press, many having played a large role in their own community's Bicentennial endeavors, reacted to the 4th of July party America threw for itself in much the same way individual citizens did, with perhaps a slightly more critical eye. On the whole, there was some astonishment, a great deal of pride and many expressions of hope that the tremendous spirit revealed over the weekend would be carried forward into the future.

Lincoln Memorial, statue of Lincoln by Daniel Chester French, Washington, D.C.

Excerpts from articles and editorials about the weekend show an almost universal reaction that it had indeed been a success.

Time—"It was an altogether fitting celebration of the 200th anniversary of America's independence, and perhaps the best part of it was that its supreme characteristics were good will, good humor, and, after a long night of paralyzing self-doubt, good feelings about the U.S."

Newsweek—". . . by and large, the nation's celebrations were as diverse and as optimistic as the history of the United States itself . . . it was a time for looking at the bright side of the American experience, past, present, and future. . . ."

U.S. News & World Report—"When it came right down to the great day, this fact stood out: Americans were getting the kind of Bicentennial they wanted—and planned for."

The Cleveland Press—"In spite of some gloomy forebodings about overselling and underenthusiasm, and about the possibilities of violence and ugly demonstrations, the birthday party was as exalting and exultant as anyone could have hoped for."

The Philadelphia Inquirer—"With joy, with warmth, with patience almost beyond imagining, Americans gave witness to America on its 200th birthday. If there were any among the United States' 214 million citizens who did not mark the day, they were hard to find and difficult to imagine."

St. Louis Globe-Democrat—"The nation as a whole and St. Louis in particular can be proud of the way in which the country's big 200th birthday bash was celebrated."

The San Diego Union—". . . Indeed what the nation needs in the next century are the qualities that Americans exhibited . . . at our big party—mature confidence, mutual respect and politeness."

Cortland (New York) Standard—"July 4, 1976, and the Bicentennial year demonstrate that people are not only aware of the Declaration of Independence but also recall and seek to renew the many instances in which Americans responded with responsibility to preserve liberty."

The (Reedsport, Oregon) Courier—"The great spectacles seen on telly from New York, Philadelphia and other metroplexes on the Fourth of July were great entertainment but the true Spirit of '76 was to be found in thousands of communities across the United States which celebrated our Bicentennial Independence Day like we did in Reedsport. . . . We looked inward to ourselves . . . and saw the American Spirit of '76."

The Washington Post—". . . Now the flag is common property again, to be stapled onto parade floats, stuck in hats and hung from front porches. The weekend was a marvelous party. It was also a moment of deep and moving reconciliation."

The New York Daily News—"New York's celebration of the nation's 200th birthday must be counted as one of the proudest and most memorable events in the city's history. . . ."

Lafayette, Ind. Journal and Courier—"From rocket's glare, to tall ships, to each region's depiction of its peoples' diverse contributions to the shaping of our whole, it brought tears, thrills and pride. A sobering, thrilling and inspiring time. Which is what it was supposed to be."

The Knickerbocker News (Albany, N.Y.)—". . . Even more importantly, many of those thousands discovered the Empire State Plaza, renewed acquaintanceship with Washington Park, were given a new understanding of the Port of Albany, where the Bicentennial Barge was docked, and learned again that downtown exists, that it can be a place of excitement and that cities—to revert to the vernacular—are 'where it's at.' "

Akron Beacon Journal—"AMERICANS, YOU'RE beautiful. For three glorious days, while blue skies prevailed over most of the nation and celebrations were held with hardly a hitch, you proved that the treasure of America is untarnished after 200 years: Her people still have faith in the patriots' dream and in each other."

The Birmingham News—"America turned the corner Sunday on a self-induced illness of the spirit and stretched its psyche in a burst of national joy and celebration."

The Evening Independent (Massilon, Ohio)—"But one thing is certain: the folks of 2076 will have to go some to outdo the 1976 celebration. We are a privileged people to have lived in the era of the Bicentennial, and we made the most of it."

The Chicago Tribune—"That grand, glorious, bell-ringing, choir singing, flag-waving, parading, skyrocketing, joyous Bicentennial is fading, reluctantly, into afterglow. And in the star-spangled euphoria that still lingers, we all, somehow, feel a little better about ourselves, about each other, and about our future as a people."

The Washington Star—"Finally, let's celebrate the warmest memory of the nation's weekend: It was the freshening of a vision that may help to sustain us when the glow of the Bicentennial fades."

The States and the
Communities
Celebrate

200 Years—
Not 200 Years Ago

54   The Centennial flag of Colorado was unfurled on each of the Rocky Mountain state's 54 peaks over 14,000 feet on August 1, 1976—Colorado Day.

The simultaneous flag-plantings occurred precisely 100 years after President Ulysses S. Grant signed the proclamation admitting Colorado as the 38th state on August 1, 1876.

Once in a Hundred. . . was the theme for "Colorado Day."

The state actually celebrated two anniversaries in the year of the nation's 200th birthday—its own Centennial of statehood and our nation's 200th year. Colorado's birthday had equal billing with the celebrations of independence.

Celebration Was Local, National

The states participated individually in the anniversary of our nation, each one celebrating its own heritage, special character and distinctive culture.

Colorado focused on its Centennial. South Dakota centered its observance on Mt. Rushmore's carved likenesses of American statesmen. Pennsylvania created the *Bicentennial Wagon Train Pilgrimage to Pennsylvania*, the Bicentennial event in which the most states participated. Virginia built a major visitor center at each corner of its Revolutionary era historic triangle—Alexandria, Charlottesville and Yorktown. Florida

developed a unique method for funding its programs, Guam paid special tribute to Vietnam refugees and Texas celebrated its cities.

There had been early agreement that the Bicentennial should be more than a celebration of the 13 original states. Several Presidential statements, as well as the recommendations in the 1970 Report to the President by the American Revolution Bicentennial Commission (ARBC), carried such a message.

(preceding pages) State flags pass in review

Bicentennial tribute at Rocky Mountains, Colorado—U.S. Senator Gary Hart and Dr. Karl Stecher atop Mt. Sherman

As Early as 1966

As early as 1966, President Lyndon B. Johnson suggested a community-level Bicentennial celebration. President Richard M. Nixon, when he addressed the ARBC in October 1969, said, "America is 50 States. America is big cities, small cities, and small towns. It is all the homes and all the hopes of 200 million people.

"That is why we want this Bicentennial to be national. It must go directly to the people and derive its strength from the people.

"And we want people all over this land to sense the greatness of this moment, to participate in it, and help us all to discover what that great spirit is."

In his message to Congress, September 1970, President Nixon supported the recommendations of the ARBC that the Bicentennial commemoration be national, involving every state, city and community.

The ARBC report and the President's message gave special emphasis to certain cities, however. Philadelphia was to be the focal point for international participation; Washington, D.C. was to set the national tone of the celebration; Boston was to explore and examine the Revolutionary roots of America; and Miami was to complete a permanent trade and cultural center by 1976.

Boston skyline

55

56 Seeds of a National Celebration

The grassroots philosophy which underlay the federal government's thinking about the Bicentennial carried the seeds of what in the end grew into a celebration that came from the hearts of people in each of America's states, territories and communities.

Early planners of the Tricentennial will have something to think about when they look back over the enormous list of community Bicentennial projects. Instead of one big show in one big city, they will discover that America's Bicentennial was celebrated in many ways by millions of Americans in thousands of communities throughout the land.

Each state contributed in its own way to the national mosaic, as American Revolution Bicentennial Administration (ARBA) Administrator John W. Warner described the Bicentennial. Each state found its own way to become part of our national exhibition.

(top) Boston and (bottom) Centennial, Wyoming celebrate

(opposite page) Model of Third Century project, Miami, Florida

How the Bicentennial Evolved

The history of state involvement in the Bicentennial reveals that an evolutionary process occurred. Although the 1966 law establishing the ARBC singled out "historic events preceding and associated with the American Revolution" as an important basis for the Bicentennial, it also suggested that federal planners consider any related activities and programs sponsored by state, local and private groups.

The ARBC ultimately voted down the idea of an international exposition in Philadelphia. It also rejected a 50 state network of Bicentennial Parks and a Bicentennial focused on a small number of designated cities.

National and international economic hard times were a significant reason for turning down these programs. Private investors as well as members of Congress did not wish to spend large amounts for programs such as an exposition or the parks.

A tight money market would later make its effect felt on state commissions debating whether to sponsor and develop major focal points as the centerpiece for their state's participation in the Bicentennial. Among the programs to feel the economic pinch were Century III in Miami, Florida and Pacific 21 in Los Angeles, California.

Olympics Go Elsewhere

Los Angeles, California and Denver, Colorado had been proposed as sites for the 1976 Summer and Winter Olympics, respectively. Los Angeles lost out to Montreal, Canada in the selection process.

Denver's story was more complicated and revolved around local issues and problems. Denver's bid, which had been endorsed by the ARBC, was voted down by the citizens of the state. They preferred to see their tax dollars used to provide facilities for local citizens rather than for services for tourists attending an international attraction.

Later some $87.5 million which would have been spent had the Olympics come to Denver was voted in a bond referendum for construction programs to improve the city for the Colorado Centennial and the nation's Bicentennial.

Raising Funds in Florida

Horse and dog racing had little to do with the Bicentennial and the Revolutionary period. In Florida, however, they had everything to do with Bicentennial planning because they provided resources needed by the Florida Bicentennial Commission. This unique state-approved funding system netted the commission $850,000 annually and altogether yielded $3.5 million which funded 350 projects.

57

58 Commissions Were Different

The planning for the celebration centered to a great degree on the state commissions.

Massachusetts, the state that gave us John and Abigail Adams, also gave the nation the first state Bicentennial commission in 1964. Virginia followed suit in 1966, and by March of 1967, just one month after the congressionally created ARBC conducted its first full meeting, the General Assembly of North Carolina voted to establish the North Carolina Bicentennial Committee. The development of the state commissions continued, and by the beginning of 1971, 11 had been funded, staffed and were in operation.

By early 1973, a state Bicentennial organization had been established in each of the 50 states, territories, the District of Columbia and the Commonwealth of Puerto Rico. People looked to these groups to show them the way to express the character of their own communities in their local celebrations.

Women Show the Way

Women's organizations had been concerned earlier that there would not be enough of their leadership in planning the Bicentennial. Events showed that a great many state commission programs were, in fact, directed by women.

Among the 24 dynamic women who provided strong leadership to their state Bicentennial commissions were Madeleine Bordallo, chairwoman, Guam; Gene Riddle Brownrigg, executive director, Texas; Peggy S. Curry, chairwoman, Wyoming; Honorable Louise Gore, chairwoman, Maryland; Rita Hendrickson, chairwoman, Alaska; Vicki Nash, executive director, Nevada; Louise L. Prickett, executive director, Delaware; Zaida E. Rosa, executive director, Puerto Rico; Gladys Warren, chairwoman and director, Oklahoma; and Jo Westpheling, chairwoman, Kentucky.

Gladys Warren, director, Oklahoma ARBC meets Marjorie Lynch, deputy administrator, ARBA

ARBA and the States

The intent to have strong state participation was reaffirmed in the 1973 law creating the American Revolution Bicentennial Administration. The nation's Bicentennial became defined as a state-by-state celebration involving every American and our friends in other countries.

The individual state commissions had differing roles and differing relationships with respect to the federal government's efforts. The idea for a national Bicentennial that stressed local celebrations evolved from these diverse local groups supported by dedicated individuals.

Following National Themes

Most state programming was structured around the three national themes which commemorated the past, present and future concerns of the nation.

Some states rediscovered their identity as they worked out ways to fund their programs, while others were successful in sponsoring and completing major national events as their contribution to the birthday.

Some states worked together for commemorative planning, as in the case of Alaska, Oregon, Washington and Hawaii. They joined to honor Captain James Cook, the English explorer who has been credited with discovering Hawaii—and blazing a maritime trail to the three continental states as well—during the same period the American Revolution was being fought.

Honoring All States

Each state and territory was honored at Mt. Rushmore during the summer of 1976. The Rushmore Festival of the States was the focus of South Dakota's role in the national celebration.

An economic interest that centered on Mt. Rushmore as a common travel destination spurred the neighboring states of Montana, Nebraska, North Dakota and Wyoming to begin their own commemoration plans, thereby forming a strong regional bond.

Mt. Rushmore, South Dakota receives official Bicentennial designation

Wagon Trains Fan Out

Perhaps the state program that involved the greatest number of other states was the Pennsylvania Bicentennial Commission's *Bicentennial Wagon Train Pilgrimage to Pennsylvania.*

This dream of Thelma Gray, president of a Pennsylvania advertising firm and originator of the program, created history in reverse, bringing replicas of the original wagon trains which had set out from Pennsylvania back to the state, which was one of the original gateways to the west. It also provided states with a program that remembered the courage and hardships of the early settlers.

The Wagon Train caravan was a thread linking many Bicentennial state commissions and communities. Over 60,000 volunteer riders from the Trail Riders' Conference and local riding groups went with the wagon train as mounted escorts and outriders. These "pony express" horsemen fanned out from state wagons to reach communities not on the main trails.

"The Bicentennial Wagon Train seemed to pull people and communities together," explained Walt Schaefer, wagonmaster and director of McCrossan Boys Ranch, Sioux Falls, South Dakota. "We found this all the way across the country. The Wagon Train was a wonderful personal experience."

(opposite page) Wagon Train at Scotts Bluff, Montana

(above) Wagon Train trails; (below) traveling from Tennessee to Virginia

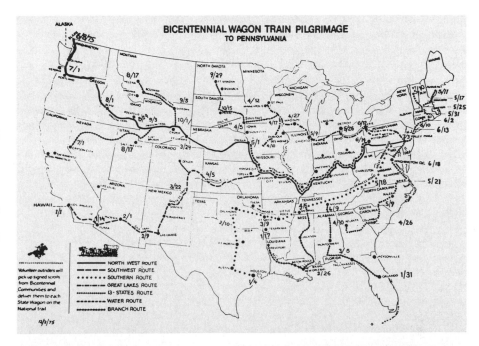

BICENTENNIAL WAGON TRAIN PILGRIMAGE
TO PENNSYLVANIA

61

64 Alliances and Western Trails

Some states formed alliances to emphasize their region's special role in the development of the nation. These alliances—the Bicentennial Council of the Thirteen Original States, the Southwest Regional Council and the Northwest Alliance—varied greatly.

It was a sense of local history that caused states to differ in the way they celebrated. States in the west, as might be expected, looked more to their Hispanic and pioneer ancestors than to Adamses, Jeffersons and Madisons. This is shown by trail reenactments in the west, such as the de Anza trek and the *Dominguez-Escalante Expedition Commemoration.*

Bicentennial symbols: Council of the Thirteen Original States; City of San Francisco; (opposite page, left) Dominguez-Escalante expedition symbol; (right) out on the Dominguez-Escalante trail

Through the Spanish Southwest

In 1974, Gordon Wallace, 66, of Prescott, Arizona decided to reenact the Dominguez-Escalante expedition to kindle appreciation for the hardships our forefathers endured in settling his part of the country.

The forefathers he meant were two young Franciscan friars—Francisco Anastasio Dominguez and Francisco Silvestre Velez de Escalante, who were sent by their ecclesiastical superiors in 1775 to establish an overland route between Santa Fe, New Mexico and Monterey, California.

Two hundred years later, the credo of Wallace's *Dominguez-Escalante Expedition Commemoration* stated: "May our coming foster a greater understanding of, and among, ourselves and our neighbors—Native, Hispanic and Anglo-American."

The expedition became a cooperative effort of the Bicentennial commissions of Colorado, New Mexico, Utah and Arizona and of the Navajo Nation.

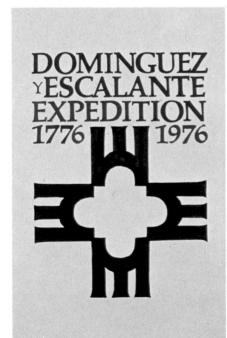

66

Crossing the Mexican Border

Another commemorative expedition was the de Anza trek. While Benedict Arnold was leading American soldiers through Maine in 1775, Juan Bautista de Anza, explorer, statesman and colonizer, was fulfilling his dream of finding a land route to California from Mexico. He set off on a 1,000 mile journey from Horcasitas in Sonora, Mexico to what is now San Francisco, California. The *presidios* at Tucson, Arizona and San Francisco were founded as a result of his journey.

The de Anza expedition reenactment was a joint effort involving the state commissions in Arizona and California and many communities along its route.

Juan Bautista de Anza trek reenactment

68 Northwest to Canada

Calgary in Alberta, Canada describes its annual international festival as "the Greatest Outdoor Show on Earth."

Its 1976 edition gave states another opportunity for Bicentennial activity. California, Colorado, Nebraska, Nevada, North Dakota, Texas, Utah, Washington and Wyoming joined the Calgary Stampede in its 1976 *Salute to the U.S. Bicentennial,* participating in rodeos, competitions, stage shows, street celebrations, parades and exhibitions.

Calgary Stampede

Trails in the East, Too

In New England, the Knox Trail Reenactment was a cooperative effort of New York, Vermont, New Hampshire and Massachusetts. Young Henry Knox had distinguished himself in 1775 by traveling some 300 miles over icy trails to bring tons of munitions to General George Washington's troops in Massachusetts.

The Bicentennial group made its trip from Fort Ticonderoga, New York to Boston over freezing roads and through snow, facing much the same weather as had confronted the original soldiers.

The Spanish heritage in the nation's founding was remembered by the Florida Bicentennial Trail, which was dedicated on July 4, 1972 at the Castillo de San Marcos. The event called to mind Florida's 400 years of dynamic growth since its Spanish and French beginnings.

Knox Trail reenactment

70 **Flags, Symbols, Parks**

Tens of thousands of national Bicentennial flags flew with U.S. flags during 1976. The distinctive Bicentennial symbol was an ever-present national reminder of the celebration. Flag and symbol were emblems which helped knit the occasion together.

Although the Bicentennial Parks concept had failed to materialize as a national program by 1973, the idea became popular with local communities in many places. As of January 1977, the Bicentennial Information Network (BINET), the ARBA's clearinghouse of Bicentennial events and projects, listed the development of just under 4,000 Bicentennial parks or natural areas as people discovered the Bicentennial parks concept for themselves.

Charleston, South Carolina, for one, created a Bicentennial park and exhibition hall. The Golden Gate Promenade, a four and one-half mile pedestrian path along San Francisco's northern waterfront, is a variation on the same theme, as is Detroit's transformation of the Old Fort Wayne Military Post in the center of the city into a recreation and education area. Oklahoma worked with its communities to establish flag plazas.

A sampling of state Bicentennial
commission symbols
(see volumes III, IV and V
for illustrations of all state symbols)

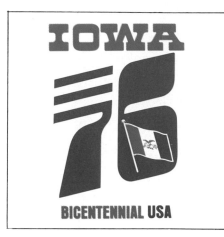

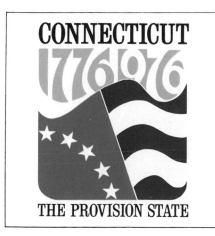

PROCLAIM LIBERTY THROUGHOUT ALL THE LAND · CALIFORNIA ·

MICHIGAN BICENTENNIAL COMMISSION

ga. 1776 1976

MARYLAND BICENTENNIAL COMMISSION
FOR THE COMMEMORATION OF THE AMERICAN REVOLUTION

1776-1976

South Dakota 1976
USA BICENTENNIAL

THE FIRST STATE

Delaware American Revolution Bicentennial

NORTH CAROLINA BICENTENNIAL

74

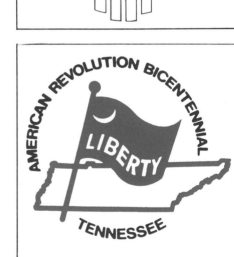

Illinois' Celebration '76

HORIZONS FESTIVAL HERITAGE '76

THE SPIRIT OF '76
In the American West!

WYOMING

1775   1783

UTAH ★ AMERICAN ★ REVOLUTION ★ BICENTENNIAL
200 YEARS YOUNG
1776 ★ 1976

**Washington State
American Revolution
Bicentennial Celebration**

A Communities Program

Communities were the focus in most states, spurred to a large extent by the ARBC's *Bicentennial Communities Program.* It provided the states with the commonality they were looking for and was a concept that offered an opportunity for everyone to participate. The program gave many state commissions the basic vehicle with which they ultimately delivered their successful celebrations.

States in the Lead

At the time the ARBC approved its national *Bicentennial Communities Program*, two states had already committed themselves to their own community programs.

In 1970, Texas was forming a community goal-setting program centered around Austin and San Antonio. Beginning in 1971, a statewide Bicentennial cities program that included Galveston, Lubbock, San Antonio, San Marcos and Temple was initiated. South Dakota, too, set in motion a statewide communities program in 1971.

First Bicentennial City

The ARBC's first step toward the *Bicentennial Communities Program* had come in 1970, when the ARBC outlined a broad Bicentennial multi-city concept in its Report to the President. The general idea was to give official recognition to certain cities which would serve as focal points in the national celebration.

In April 1971, Niagara Falls, New York became the first city to seek official designation on the basis of its Rainbow Center project, an impressive urban renewal plan. A delegation led by the Mayor, E. Dent Lackey, and U.S. Representative Henry P. Smith

presented the Rainbow Center project to the ARBC.

The complicated ARBC criteria, in effect at that time for official recognition as a national program, were met, and a formal application was submitted. Despite reservations by some commission members that the program seemed more urban renewal than historic, official recognition was accorded to Niagara Falls on December 10, 1971. It became the first national Bicentennial City.

Cities Become Communities

Other cities were quick to follow Niagara Falls' footsteps. In July 1972, Mayor-President W. W. Dumas of Baton Rouge, Louisiana submitted an ambitious 50 project proposal to the ARBC and asked for official recognition as a Bicentennial City.

The application was discussed at an ARBC meeting on September 8, 1972. It was apparent to the ARBC members that they had not established uniform guidelines for evaluating such applications and administering a nationwide program for cities. Therefore, they could not act on the application. A motion was carried approving the concept, but designation of Bicentennial Cities was deferred until guidelines were adopted and procedures established.

Guidelines were developed by the ARBC staff working closely with the U.S. Conference of Mayors, the National League of Cities, the National Governors' Conference and the National Association of Counties. State commissions were consulted and contributed greatly to the program as it was finally adopted.

On March 26, 1973, the *Bicentennial Communities Program* was officially launched. The term "communities" was chosen rather than "cities" to allow

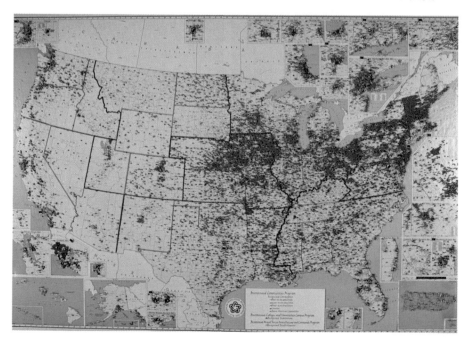

participation by all political groupings with an independently elected government. Later, the program was broadened even further to include unincorporated areas. Still later, two similar programs were set up to cover colleges and universities and military installations.

The Four Step Procedure

With streamlined procedures, a four step application and approval process was adopted as follows. (1) Organize a special Bicentennial planning committee representing the entire community. (2) Develop programs in as many of the three national theme areas as possible: *Heritage '76*—remembrance of the past; *Festival USA*—celebration of our cultures; *Horizons '76*—preparing for our third century. In addition, one community project had to provide a "lasting reminder" of the community's

Bicentennial activity. A community then (3) had to obtain the approval of its chief elected official and (4) submit its application to the ARBC through its state Bicentennial commission.

Overwhelming Response

The *Bicentennial Communities Program* made its debut and was endorsed officially at the U.S. Conference of Mayors' annual meeting, June 18, 1973, in San Francisco. Overwhelming community response followed.

On July 3, 1973, Counselor to the President and White House liaison for the Bicentennial effort, Anne L. Armstrong, announced recognition of eight Bicentennial Communities. Thirty-five months later to the day, on June 3, 1976, ARBA Administrator John W. Warner announced official recognition of the final 202 Bicentennial Communities.

The total number of official Bicentennial designations had reached 11,739, encompassing some 12,566 different communities.

77

(below left) Red Stick Monument, Baton Rouge, Louisiana; (right) fireworks over Niagara Falls

(opposite page) Official ARBA Bicentennial Communities locator map as of July 4, 1976

78 Boston Lights the Fuse—Again

The city that lit the fuse of the American Revolution prepared a civic, cultural and economic explosion whose aim was to set off a much-needed urban renaissance in the last quarter of the 20th century.

Such was the idea of Mayor Kevin H. White of Boston in May 1972 as he laid out preliminary plans for Boston 200. During 1969 and 1970, the mayor had been involved in planning for a national Bicentennial exposition. Now he was committing himself and his city to a new concept for the Bicentennial observance. "We have rejected the traditional fair ground approach and have declared the new exposition grounds to be the city itself," the mayor said. "This approach can be summarized in a phrase, 'The City Is the Exhibit.' Its implementation relies not so much on new construction, but rather on what already exists—our historic resources, our institutions and our people."

Following Boston's Initiative

As Boston planned, so did the nation. There was a burgeoning community feeling about the Bicentennial across the land at the time Boston was making its plans public. This happened in cities that had been part of the American Revolution—Charleston, South Carolina; Savannah, Georgia; Alexandria and Yorktown, Virginia; Lexington and Concord, Massachusetts; and New Bern, North Carolina. It was also happening in places with no roots in the Revolution—Andalusia, Alabama; Shaniko, Oregon; and Akron, Nebraska.

Just as Bostonians used the Bicentennial as an opportunity to bring changes of lasting importance to their city, so too did thousands of other communities across the country.

(top and center) Bicentennial weekend 1976 in Chicago, Illinois; (lower left) Silver Eagle regatta, San Francisco; (lower right) restoration in Charleston, South Carolina

Varied Community Efforts

San Antonio, Texas chose to redevelop Alamo Plaza, the area where the mission compound once stood. Biloxi, Mississippi created a Seafood Trail, an eight mile tour of seafood factories, old homes and other historic points important to its local seafood industry. Citizens of Hartford, Wisconsin established a fully equipped emergency service squad as their project.

Billings, Montana carried out an energy conservation demonstration; Duluth, Minnesota, a historical building identification project; Greeley, Colorado, a botanical gardens and Centennial Trail; Indianapolis, Indiana, the Lockerbie Square Restoration project; Trumbull, Connecticut, *From Valley Forge to Freedom: The Story of a Black Patriot,* a book about a distinguished resident of the community.

A 44 foot steel sculpture, *Keeper of the Plains,* was raised in Wichita, Kansas in memory of the Plains Indians, stage one of a larger project honoring Native Americans.

When asked why Tabor, South Dakota, a town of 400 people in the "Heart of Czech Dakota-land," celebrated both the Bicentennial and the 104th anniversary of the town's founding by Czech immigrants, town Bicentennial planner Laddie Kostel answered: "It can perhaps be described as the ability and willingness of people to keep alive the very things that have made them what they are, and as long as the people of Tabor can say 'that is my heritage and my history and my town' it will never fade."

(top) Beloit, Kansas schoolhouse; (lower left) Bicentennial Community exhibit, Cupertino, California; (lower right) oral history at Snyder, Wyoming

80

(clockwise, beginning upper left) Puerto Rico street celebration; Honolulu, Hawaii; Big Horn, Wyoming; movie actor Robert Redford at burial ceremonies for mountainman John "Jeremiah" Johnson, near Cody, Wyoming; Tabor, South Dakota; Czech days in South Dakota; Honorable Ben W. Fortson, Jr., Georgia secretary of state; (middle) flag-raising sign in Big Horn, Wyoming

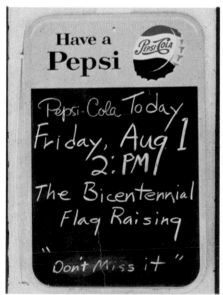

Centennial Celebrates Twice

In 1976, Centennial, Wyoming celebrated its 100th birthday and the Bicentennial at the same time. The citizens of Centennial had three projects: move the old Union Pacific depot to a new location and turn it into a museum; clean up the community dump; and celebrate Centennial Grassroots Days, the birthday party of the only community named Centennial in the United States. At the Bicentennial Community designation ceremonies, which John W. Warner attended, Centennial's 150 residents turned loose 1,000 helium balloons, each with a message about the Bicentennial. The cards were found in places as far away as Nebraska, Kansas, Missouri and Kentucky. One balloon was picked up many hundreds of miles away in Piscataway, New Jersey, only 23 hours after it was set free.

Neighborhoods Were Active

The communities program worked because it reached into neighborhoods and did not stop at city hall officials.

For example, Allen, Oklahoma's Bicentennial community program was led by 14 year old Johnny Oglesbee.

Neighborhoods in Chicago put that city's program on the map, while blocks in the Latino sections of Los Angeles paid tribute to their cultures.

New faces leading community efforts encouraged other new faces to appear.

Restoration at Centennial, Wyoming

82 Jefferson's Charlottesville

Michael Gleason of Charlottesville, Virginia is 31 years old and able to look back on his six years as chairman of the Albemarle-Charlottesville Bicentennial Commission with pride. One of the three statewide information centers is now in Charlottesville. Gleason had worked hard to get it there.

The young people in his town can point out the Revolutionary War cemeteries they cleaned up. And as a lasting reminder of Charlottesville's Bicentennial program, the town produced a film, *Mr. Jefferson's Legacy*.

Why did Michael Gleason work so hard on the Bicentennial? "It was a once-in-a-lifetime experience," he says, and doubts "there will be anything like it until the Tricentennial."

The idea of working within time limits toward a completion date of July 1976 was part of the magic of the Bicentennial. Communities had a target to work toward. Americans seemed to want to do something special for the Bicentennial and to do it by or during 1976.

Intangible Benefits, Mainly

There were few tangible benefits from ARBC/ARBA official recognition—a certificate of recognition, a presentation ceremony, a Bicentennial flag and permission to display that flag and use the Bicentennial symbol. There was no commitment of financial assistance. Relatively little was offered in return for what was freely given.

This did not diminish the generous outpouring of spirit everywhere.

Parke S. Rouse, Jr., director of the Virginia Independence Bicentennial Commission, remarked at the end of the communities program in March 1976, "Now that the Bicentennial Community and Bicentennial Campus programs have ended, I want to congratulate ARBA on this excellent concept. It did a great deal to get the counties, cities, and colleges of Virginia interested and involved in the Bicentennial."

(top) New Western Virginia Bicentennial Center at Charlottesville; (left) new Yorktown Victory Center, Virginia; (right) restoration of the Lyceum in Alexandria as the George Washington Northern Virginia Bicentennial Center

College Communities

As Bicentennial preparations continued, the *Bicentennial Communities Program* was broadened to include college and university campuses and Armed Forces installations.

Colleges and universities could become Bicentennial Campuses beginning November 1974. Until then, college students had shown little interest in the Bicentennial. The combination of the Vietnam War and Watergate had turned them against federal programs in general.

However, by the end of 1974 students began to support the Bicentennial as a new cause. They were adamantly opposed to any kind of Bicentennial "made in Washington," but showed a desire to use the year 1976 as a target to accomplish campus projects that had merit.

Recognizing that the concerns of college communities were in many cases different from the towns and cities in which they were located, the ARBA issued *Bicentennial Colleges and Universities Campuses Program* guidelines. Endorsed by the state commissions, they encouraged joint campus/community projects.

Alabama Campus First

The University of Alabama became the first Bicentennial Campus on November 8, 1974. Nine hundred and twenty-nine colleges and universities were to become part of the program during its 19 month life.

Some colleges established *Heritage '76* studies programs. Others put together dissertations on the basic concerns of early America. One college wrote a history of its earliest days.

Many schools studied the philosophy of the American Revolution and events of the past 200 years. Still others sponsored lectures about America's early history and the nation's relationships with the rest of the world.

Many Different Projects

Many other observances were scheduled in colleges and universities, large and small. For instance, at Bowling Green State University in Ohio, a one room schoolhouse was moved to the campus and made into a museum. At Salt Lake City, the University of Utah produced a musical version of Sidney Kingsley's play, *The Patriots.* At Colby College in Maine, a Bicentennial exhibit on *Maine Forms of American Architecture* was displayed during the summer of 1976. West Virginia University sponsored an international symposium on 18th century journalism.

84 Armed Forces Join In

The Armed Forces were officially invited by the ARBA in December 1974 to join the *Bicentennial Communities Program* through a special *Bicentennial Armed Forces Installations and Commands Program.* Word came back from each branch—affirmative.

The first Bicentennial Installations and Commands were announced on Armed Forces Day, May 14, 1975. Thirteen months later, official ARBA recognition had gone to 599 Military Installations and Commands in 49 states, the District of Columbia, Guam and the Commonwealth of Puerto Rico. Eighty-six were in 18 foreign countries.

(top) United States Armed Forces Bicentennial Band premiere concert, Kennedy Center, Washington, D.C.; (below) Armed Forces posters and insignias

(opposite page, clockwise, beginning upper left) 1876 Ceremonial Unit at the presidio *in San Francisco; exhibit at the Naval Museum, Washington, D.C.; Navy retrieval of Revolutionary War cannons; Air Force chorus at the Alamo, San Antonio, Texas*

Adak, Alaska and the Navy

Borne on winds of treeless hills—
On gulls as white as snow—
On tundra-covered rocks and rills
A future starts to grow.

> —stanza from *Adak's Bicentennial Poem,* by Lieutenant Commander Jerry Jacobson

The westernmost community in the nation, Adak, Alaska, now has a forest of 2,500 trees, thanks to Navy Bicentennial Commands at the Adak Naval Station.

The complement at the station, together with the island's civilians, make up a population of only 6,000. But this remote, close-knit community planned 21 Bicentennial projects, including a toy collection for Alaskan Indians, a museum and park and a wooden nickel sale.

It was the forestry project that stole the show, though. The island was barren and windswept except for a dozen and a half or so trees brought in over the years.

Careful planning led up to the preparations for the new forest. Nine military and civilian representatives joined in attending a two week course on plant ecology. Now Adak Island has a forest which hopefully will survive and grow for generations.

More from the Navy

The 219 Navy Bicentennial Commands, as the Navy's Bicentennial communities were called, consisted of ships, shore installations and aircraft and helicopter squadrons in the United States, as well as in such places as **Morocco, England, Panama, Taiwan, Greece, Bermuda and Scotland.**

U.S. Armed Forces celebrate: (left) Fort Benning, Georgia; (right) Bicentennial symbol on Air Force plane; (below) Fort Lewis, Washington; (opposite page, top) Fort Carson, Colorado; (bottom) restoration of Fort Putnam, West Point, New York

Funding State Efforts

As state commissions transformed their ideas into working plans, their need for support from the private sector and federal agencies increased. The demand placed on the ARBC to coordinate state programming with related federal agencies led to the opening and staffing of 10 regional offices. Congress supported the ARBC's efforts to help state Bicentennial commissions by appropriating funds for their administrative costs.

In 1972, $45,000 was appropriated for each state and $30,000 for the Commonwealth of Puerto Rico, the territories and the District of Columbia. That same amount was appropriated in 1973, except that the District of Columbia was given $45,000. In 1974, 1975 and 1976, Congress appropriated $25,000 per entity for use toward the administrative costs of the official Bicentennial organizations that helped state and community programs operate.

State Legislatures Help

Following this federal financial commitment and the cancellation of the concept of a single city exposition, many legislatures appropriated state funds for their commissions to finance programs and projects. These funds gave the celebration ever-increasing momentum.

While the total amount of state funding cannot be determined until the Bicentennial period ends in 1983, it is impressive to note that about $25 million in state funds had been committed by mid-1976.

Local Government, Private, Funds

A U.S. Conference of Mayors' survey of 444 representative cities, completed in October 1976, showed that while some officials complained about the lack of federal funds for community

Bicentennial programs, they made up for it by turning to local public and private resources. The cities surveyed were spending $141.5 million on 546 Bicentennial projects, of which 69 percent came from local governments and private contributors.

ARBC, ARBA Funds

At the same time, the ARBC was pushing ahead with its commemorative medals program, with which it was able to provide a further financial boost to states and communities.

Revenues derived from the sale of congressionally-authorized ARBC and ARBA medals struck by the U.S. Mint were also made available to the states through a matching grants-in-aid program. The sum of $40,000 to each state and $30,000 each to the territories, District of Columbia and Commonwealth of Puerto Rico, for a total of $2.15 million, gave the state programs a much-needed shot in the arm. As a result, hundreds of projects and activities were undertaken by the state commissions. This initial grants-in-aid program was started in 1973 and was followed by three total yearly grants of $2.2 million, for an overall total of $8.75 million. Without doubt, this ambitious program provided much encouragement to the states and other entities, and, in many cases, much of the money filtered down to local Bicentennial programs.

Federal Funds for States

The early success of this program—particularly the fact that each federal dollar was matched by almost four dollars from either state, local or private funds—helped to bring about another major funding program for the states. Public Law 93–179, enacted December 11, 1973, created the ARBA and also authorized a program which provided

$11 million in federally appropriated funds to finance a $200,000 matching grants-in-aid program for each of the states, territories, District of Columbia and Commonwealth of Puerto Rico.

Funding assistance during the lives of the ARBC and the ARBA came to a total of over $500,000 for each state, territory, the District of Columbia and the Commonwealth of Puerto Rico.

Not So Easy for Communities

By law each state commission received funds from the federal government. However, Bicentennial Communities were not so blessed. Official community designation did not mean that money automatically poured in. Nevertheless, efforts at national and state levels did help communities seeking financial assistance. In a few states—Louisiana and Illinois, for example—a community had to have put its Bicentennial aims and needs together and applied for and received the official Bicentennial Community designation in order to share in the funding authorized by Congress for those states' Bicentennial programs.

Efforts to define local goals within the Bicentennial framework often led to tangible community benefits. The old schoolhouse which everybody had been meaning to restore for years would now get some attention. The information center for tourists which had been talked about for years was finished in time for Bicentennial visitors. Accommodations directories were written; community parks were landscaped; school bands got new uniforms.

Louisville's Blocks, for Instance

In Louisville, Kentucky, Mayor Harvey Sloane and 10 city departments formed a partnership with both citizens and businesses to bring quick improvement to the city's environment. The Louisville *Bicentennial Block Project* resulted in the renovation of six residential blocks. Donations in labor and supplies totaled as much as $10,000 per block, and volunteers put in an average of 1,100 hours work on each.

The Jaycees had helped launch the program, and the Navy's Seabees donated their skills on a regular basis. Other volunteer groups also helped.

Mayor Sloane summed up: "Volunteer groups have worked with residents in the 'barnraising' spirit of colonial days. City employees have given special services to block residents. And the residents have built a new pride in their neighborhoods, and new relationships with the neighbors on their Bicentennial block."

In Oklahoma City, Oklahoma, a number of trade associations and businesses, including contractors, made the construction of a downtown Bicentennial Plaza their special Bicentennial contribution. The plaza's centerpiece is a sculpture depicting the nation's first land rush—in 1889, when Oklahoma City, five other towns and several thousand farms were staked out a few hours after the starting gun was fired.

(top two) Louisville, Kentucky street clean-up; (third) Greenville, Tennessee restoration; (fourth) Devils Lake, Wisconsin rebuilding

Donated funds, services and goods met $175,000 of the $200,000 needed. A $25,000 grant from the state Bicentennial commission made up the difference.

Funds for Bicentennial Jobs

An additional source of federal funding for state Bicentennial projects came from the U.S. Department of Commerce through Title X of the Public Works and Economic Development Act of 1965.

Altogether, 116 Bicentennial projects qualified for just over $16 million in federal grants under Title X, which concentrates federal development assistance in areas with high unemployment. The projects were chosen by the Department of Commerce from applications approved by the ARBA. The money was used for projects that created jobs.

Community benefits included $2.4 million for the Liberty State Park in Hudson County, New Jersey; $1.2 million for a Bicentennial transportation loop in Vermont; $295,680 for the Woodward-East renaissance, a Black community development project in Detroit, Michigan; $185,000 for the Heritage Center complex, Navajo Nation, Arizona; $150,000 for the Monroe County Courthouse renovation in Mississippi; $100,000 for renovation of Standing Rock Sioux historical sites, Standing Rock Sioux tribe, North Dakota; $60,000 for a water and sewer project on the Wind River Indian Reservation in Wyoming; and $96,200 for six projects in Puerto Rico, ranging from town improvements and recreation centers to the establishment of a sugar industry museum in Guayama.

89

Symbol Displayed Everywhere

The national Bicentennial symbol was on the official recognition document each of the Bicentennial Communities received. It also showed up on cornerstones, monuments, bumper stickers, posters, certificates of achievement, tour guides and maps. It was even displayed in a red, white and blue flower bed at the Peace Arch in Blaine, Washington.

In Holly, Michigan, laying 1,000 bricks to reproduce the symbol was a lot like putting together a huge jigsaw puzzle, according to the two determined men who did it.

Jess "Cherokee" O'Bryan, a master bricklayer and precision diamond cutter, teamed with Dr. Henry Raskin, who first thought of the symbol as appropriate for Battle Alley, a 19th century-style shopping area.

The red, white and blue bricks used to form the symbol were specially ordered. Each carries the name of the Holly resident who bought it for from $2 to $5 to pay for the ambitious project's cost. A yearly Name Signing Day is planned to keep the names legible, and a master chart will help locate each name.

As Seen from the Sky

Rosemary Wilkins and Vicki Prelesnik, two young Santa Ana, California mothers—one British and the other American—painted the Bicentennial symbol on the helicopter pad on top of the building which housed the office of the Santa Ana Bicentennial Committee.

Says Gene Moriarty, chairman of the committee, "Anyone flying over Santa Ana will recognize us as a Bicentennial Community."

Common Themes

Display of the Bicentennial symbol did provide tangible evidence of tens of thousands of projects throughout the nation.

In reviewing all these projects, it is interesting to examine the threads of common interest—restorations, time capsules, parks, decorative painting of fire hydrants, traveling exhibits.

Bicentennial symbol on television, roof tops, teeshirts, balloons, airplanes, letters and buses

92

Restorations Are Popular

Restorations were perhaps the most popular of community programs. The BINET listed just over 3,600 restoration projects.

The *Bicentennial Times,* the ARBA's monthly newspaper, reported on many of these restorations, which ranged from face-liftings for important historic buildings and homes to the experience of one small town in Ohio.

The village of Columbiana, which calls itself the "biggest little town in Ohio," finished a $75,000 Bicentennial project without—as reported in the local weekly newspaper—ever holding a committee meeting, electing a committee chairman or receiving a nickel in matching grant money.

The Columbiana Historical Society spread the word that it was looking for a log cabin or log house to restore as a *Heritage* project. The society wanted to commemorate Columbiana's beginnings in the early 1800's as one of the Western Reserve villages.

The Columbiana Boiler Company happened to have such a log house on its parking lot and was getting ready to tear it down. The Bookwalter family of Columbiana offered a site for it on the village square. The house was moved to the site, materials were rounded up and a foundation was dug.

When completed, the log house was turned over to the historical society as a museum.

(top left) Restoration, Des Moines, Iowa; (lower left) St. Augustine, Florida

(opposite page, top) Washington, D.C.; (middle) Central City, Colorado; (lower left) Sitka, Alaska; (lower right) Alexandria, Virginia

Restoring for Use

The purpose of most restoration projects was to give modern day usefulness to sound old buildings. The Virginia Independence Bicentennial Commission, for example, restored the historic Lyceum in Alexandria. Built in 1839 as a library and lecture-concert hall, the Lyceum now serves as one of the three new state Bicentennial information and exhibit centers.

An old railroad depot in Steamboat Springs, Colorado became a museum, art gallery and community center. The elegant Ohio Theater in Columbus regained its 1928 grandeur and is now used as a performing arts center and home for the Columbus Symphony Orchestra.

In Ogden, Utah, the state Bicentennial commission gave $150,000 to the city to restore its historic railroad depot. The depot now has a transportation museum that shows Ogden's part in the growth of rail transportation—the first of the transcontinental rail lines joined near Ogden in 1869.

Auburn University in Auburn, Alabama turned the town's oldest public building into a university chapel. The structure was originally built in 1850 as the First Presbyterian Church of Auburn.

New Harmony, Indiana

One of the most ambitious restoration projects of all was the $18 million, two year restoration and economic recovery effort in New Harmony, Indiana, where Robert Owen's utopian community had been established in 1825. Many buildings from the community's early years had survived; more than 50 were chosen as important enough to restore. Thrall's Opera House, built in 1822 and used by Indiana college and university theatrical groups, was among them.

Traveling Exhibitions

Community-by-community, the celebration gained an important dimension from such nationally recognized touring events as the Freedom Train and the *Armed Forces Bicentennial Exhibit Vans.* The vans, for instance, focused on small cities and towns and appeared in over 1,000 communities. In many cases, the roadshows served as catalysts for local projects.

Freedom Train in Ohio

On the three day weekend that the Freedom Train was in Archbold, Ohio, the town's 3,160 citizens stopped everything to celebrate. The local Bicentennial committee sold over 35,000 tickets to the Freedom Train to residents in a 14 county area.

Most of the population of this midwestern town wore authentic 1776 costumes when they took part in several events, including a reenactment of the signing of the Declaration of Independence. For that, townspeople dressed up like the original signers. Actor and comedian Robert Preston gave a narration of Benjamin Franklin in Paris, and a 180 member local chorus sang the *Battle Hymn of the Republic.*

Max Smith, owner of radio station WHFD in Archbold, was the prime mover behind their 72 hour celebration. He said afterward that some 52,000 people turned out and that at one time the line of people waiting to visit the Freedom Train stretched for four miles.

Mariachi in El Paso

A Japanese folk dance troupe went to Milwaukee, and Mexican mariachi groups performed in El Paso. Italians danced the tarantella to tambourines in Los Angeles.

These performers were originally part of the *Festival of American Folklife* in Washington, D.C., sponsored by the Smithsonian Institution, the National Park Service and the ARBA. Many of the festival's groups and individual performers toured the country to bring their excitement to some 61 communities.

In some communities, performers joined local festivals, as in the case of *Summerfest* in Milwaukee. Other communities created festivals around the tours. Two city-wide festivals in Philadelphia featured performances by touring groups. A festival in Lincoln, Nebraska hosted German performers with picnics and dances in small neighborhood communities. Italians were honored at the New Orleans Piazza d'Italia. In Wichita, Kansas, students from Ghana joined the local Bicentennial commission in planning Ghanaian participation in the *Black Arts and Heritage Festival.*

The American Freedom Train

Fire Plugs and Fairs

Ruth von Karowsky encouraged 400 citizens, aged 9 to 79, to paint the 4,800 fire plugs of South Bend, Indiana so they resembled Revolutionary War soldiers. The sale of "I Love South Bend" buttons helped pay for the project.

Next in line came Washington, D.C., Tennessee, Wisconsin, Idaho and West Virginia, where fire plugs became Betsy Ross, Revolutionary soldiers and historical flags.

Students in Enfield, Connecticut staged a Bicentennial Fair featuring colonial games and an 18th century fashion show.

Other colonial fairs occurred in American Samoa, Georgia, Minnesota and New Jersey.

Seward, Nebraska built a time capsule large enough to hold a 1976 Chevrolet Vega and murals painted by area students.

Other states also had time capsules as Bicentennial projects—Maryland, Delaware, the Virgin Islands and Rhode Island. In fact, every state was given a time capsule by the Reynolds Metals Company in which they could keep state Bicentennial documents for posterity.

Local Chapters Active

Many of the Bicentennial's major concepts were reflected in community projects by local chapters of national organizations.

Leaders of 257 national organizations committed their members to participate in the Bicentennial. They encouraged local chapters to support local projects. Where there were no ongoing local programs, national organizations suggested that their members help start them. Members of the United States Jaycees, the National Conference on Social Welfare, the Boy Scouts of America and the Disabled American Veterans worked actively on Bicentennial projects at the community level.

(opposite page, left and upper right) Fireplugs in South Bend, Indiana; (lower right) on the river in San Antonio, Texas

(this page, clockwise, beginning at the top) Freedom Folksingers at the Alamo, Texas; time capsule burial, Oklahoma City, Oklahoma; U.S. Army time capsule, Little Rock, Arkansas; Reynolds Metals time capsule; Tulip Festival, Pella, Iowa

A Unique Problem

As most states prepared to unfold their major events in 1976, a few faced a unique problem. Celebrations in the states of Washington and Kentucky came into focus before the Bicentennial year.

Spokane, Washington had hosted *Expo '74,* an environment-oriented international exposition in 1974, so by 1976 Washington state had already successfully presented a major Bicentennial effort and had received its greatest attention from American and foreign visitors.

Kentucky marked the Bicentennial of its founding in 1974 with the 100th running of the Kentucky Derby and a series of local historical events. Although the state Bicentennial commission outlined projects which would continue through 1976, no other was as memorable to Kentucky as the Centennial Derby, which was attended by Britain's Princess Margaret and Lord Snowden.

Expo '74, *Spokane, Washington*

Native American Communities

States with large Indian populations worked to include Native American communities in their Bicentennial programs.

The Chitimachas of Louisiana, better known as the Lake Indians, preserved a patch of wilderness for an overnight campground and developed a roadside park and picnic area. The tribe, numbering 400, also built a new tribal center as a Bicentennial effort.

The Shoshone tribe in Wyoming began a water and sewer project, while the Navajo Nation in Arizona completed an improved irrigation system.

The Bicentennial was providing a new insight into the status and problems of Native Americans. As the nation celebrated its 200th year, they hoped the Bicentennial would be instrumental in drawing attention to such problems as treaties, water and natural resources and the need for a better standard of living, better health facilities and better housing and education.

(top) Plains Indian tribe in Oklahoma at Bicentennial Community program; (bottom) dedication of the Chief Joseph Monument on U.S. Highway 60 near Tonkawa, Oklahoma

100 From the Potomac to the Pacific

Place and time had a great effect on the differing complexions of the Bicentennial in Washington, D.C. and Guam.

Washington, D.C. had its role as "state," city and seat of the federal government. The federal influence far outweighed the city's role: a National Visitors Center was built, a new museum—the Smithsonian's National Air and Space Museum—opened, the *Festival of American Folklife* kept going throughout the Bicentennial summer.

Well aware of the city's unique status, the D.C. Bicentennial commission staged its own city celebration, which has become an annual festival involving local foods, crafts and music. The District group also conducted a program, Salute to the States, that by the end of 1976 had honored each state and territory.

The business community rallied behind Happy Birthday, USA!, a nonprofit citizen's group which was formed to give Washington and the nation a 4th of July weekend parade and fireworks display which will long be remembered.

Far across the Pacific in Guam, where America's day begins (the island is beyond the International Date Line), "independence" activities began in March 1975 when the Vietnam War ended.

Approximately 150,000 Vietnamese refugees bound for mainland USA were taken first to Guam. Guamanians greeted these latest immigrants with copies of the Declaration of Independence printed in Vietnamese. The Guam Bicentennial commission had suggested that each village adopt a group of refugees and make it welcome. The villagers agreed and immediately won the friendship of these newest arrivals.

City celebration 1974, Washington, D.C.

Everybody Celebrated America

"What has been most extraordinary about our Bicentennial," said John Warner as he cut a ribbon at a ceremony in Stuttgart, Arkansas, "is that it is the people of this country working in their own communities who have created the Bicentennial spirit."

Warner traveled over 300,000 miles, visiting each state and territory at least once between the time he became administrator on April 11, 1974 through the 4th of July, 1976. He observed that hardly a community failed to discover and celebrate some aspect of our history or culture.

Each state, territory, commonwealth and community celebrated in its own way in its own time—but all celebrated America.

All contributed individually to the beautiful and typically American mosaic we call the Bicentennial. The result was a celebration of all the states, united together, to commemorate 200 years of the United States.

(top) Dedication at Stuttgart, Arkansas; (bottom) Shickley, Nebraska

A Past to Remember

Tempers ran hot in the chill December air. Thousands of Bostonians swarmed to the waterfront shouting, "Boston Harbor a teapot tonight." Small bands disguised themselves as Indians and crept aboard three British ships moored at Griffin's Wharf. Into the tide went 10,000 pounds sterling worth of East India Company tea.

Although marked by a spirit of masquerade and adventure, the Boston Tea Party was no prank. It was a deliberate gesture of defiance by a group of patriots willing to fight for their ideals.

George III was furious. The colonies had been relatively quiet since the repeal in 1770 of the hated Townshend taxes—all except that levied on tea. The King had insisted "there must always be one tax to keep up the right" to tax.

It was this "right" that was being rejected by the colonists—unless they were represented. The British Crown had cleverly scaled the tea tax so that the price of tea with the tax was still less than that of smuggled tea. The colonists

would "acknowledge" the Crown's right to tax because they would save money—so the reasoning went. But the colonists refused to put a price tag on freedom. They dumped the tea in protest.

The protest in 1773 in Boston Harbor provided clear evidence that the colonists did not take lightly their opposition to taxes imposed without their consent. The Crown reacted quickly with harsh measures—including a blockade of the harbor.

More than two years were to pass before the 56 representatives of the 13 colonies, assembled in Philadelphia for the Second Continental Congress, pledged "their lives, their fortunes and their sacred honor" to the cause of freedom by signing the Declaration of Independence. But on that cold December night in Boston Harbor, the American Revolution became inevitable.

Concord Bridge, Concord, Massachusetts, April 19, 1975

Replica of 1773 Boston Tea Party ship, Beaver, *Boston Harbor*

The Script That Grew . . . and Grew

It was also inevitable that Americans 200 years later would commemorate the anniversary of this momentous event.

On December 16, 1973, a crowd of more than 20,000 swarmed around Boston Harbor to witness a reenactment of the 1773 tea dumping. Unlike the original event, this Tea Party had been carefully scripted—in this case by Boston 200, the Bicentennial planning office established by Boston Mayor Kevin H. White. It was the culmination of a weekend of lectures, exhibits, street fairs, concerts and even a Tea Party Ball. The crowd braved freezing temperatures and Boston's first snow of the season.

The determination to protest that provoked the original Tea Party was not absent at the official reenactment. Some 30 actors and local militiamen in knickers and ruffles lowered into the water empty tea boxes from the *Beaver II,* a reproduction of the original brig, built by the Salada Tea Company. As they did, a militiaman shouted, "Down with King George!" Protestors mingling in the crowd shouted back: "Down with King Richard." They meant the incumbent President, Richard M. Nixon. When the actors departed, the People's Bicentennial Commission, a private antiestablishment organization protesting oil company profits as well as Presidential conduct, dumped empty oil barrels over the side of the *Beaver II.*

No one cause had a monopoly there. A conservative group from Philadelphia cruised in a yacht labeled, "Taxation Is Theft." The Church of Scientology distributed leaflets. People carrying banners ranging from "Gay American Revolution" to "Long Live the Struggle of Greek Students" milled among the crowd. The Disabled American

Veterans, wearing Indian costumes in imitation of the colonists, staged their own reenactment. The Boston Indian Council, claiming defamation of character, protested.

In Washington, D.C., Anne L. Armstrong, counselor to the President and White House liaison for the official Bicentennial, said gamely, "The spirit of America is in its diversity."

She was to make history on her own in 1976 by becoming the first woman ambassador to Britain's Court of St. James.

Boston Tea Party reenactment, December 16, 1973

108

Boston Tea Party reenactment,
December 16, 1973

Official Changes Brew in Washington

While Boston 200 was launching its highly successful Bicentennial program with the Tea Party Weekend, major changes in the national Bicentennial planning effort were brewing in Washington. On December 11, 1973, Congress replaced the American Revolution Bicentennial Commission (ARBC) with the American Revolution Bicentennial Administration (ARBA). Although the ARBC had encountered many difficulties in the early years of Bicentennial planning, its achievements had been considerable. The ARBC had established the three basic themes for the official Bicentennial, along with criteria for recognizing national programs and the very successful *Bicentennial Communities Program.* Development of a number of other major programs within each of the themes rounded out the ARBC's legacy.

The Words of History

One of the most successful of the programs in the ARBC *Heritage '76* theme area—the *National Historic Records Program*—was officially recognized on May 16, 1972. This effort to locate, identify and preserve records of the nation's colonial era and succeeding 200 year history had been recommended by Dr. Alexander Wall of the American Association for State and Local History; Dr. T. Harry Williams, Organization of American Historians; Dr. Thomas Cochran, American Historical Association; Dr. George Haskins, American Society for Legal History; and Charles E. Lee, Society of American Archivists.

The final result of this effort was a nationwide archival program that will endure long beyond the Bicentennial.

On December 22, 1974, President Gerald R. Ford signed legislation expanding the mandate of the 40 year old National Historic Publications Commission to include the objectives of the ARBC's *National Historic Records Program.*

Commission Provided Foundation

The ARBC had been productive, and when John W. Warner took up his duties as the administrator of the ARBA on April 11, 1974, he recognized its important contribution: "Although the hour is late, much valuable work has been done. There has been laid a valuable foundation by the labors of many tireless, selfless persons, on which we can continue to build."

Mount Vernon, Virginia, home of George Washington

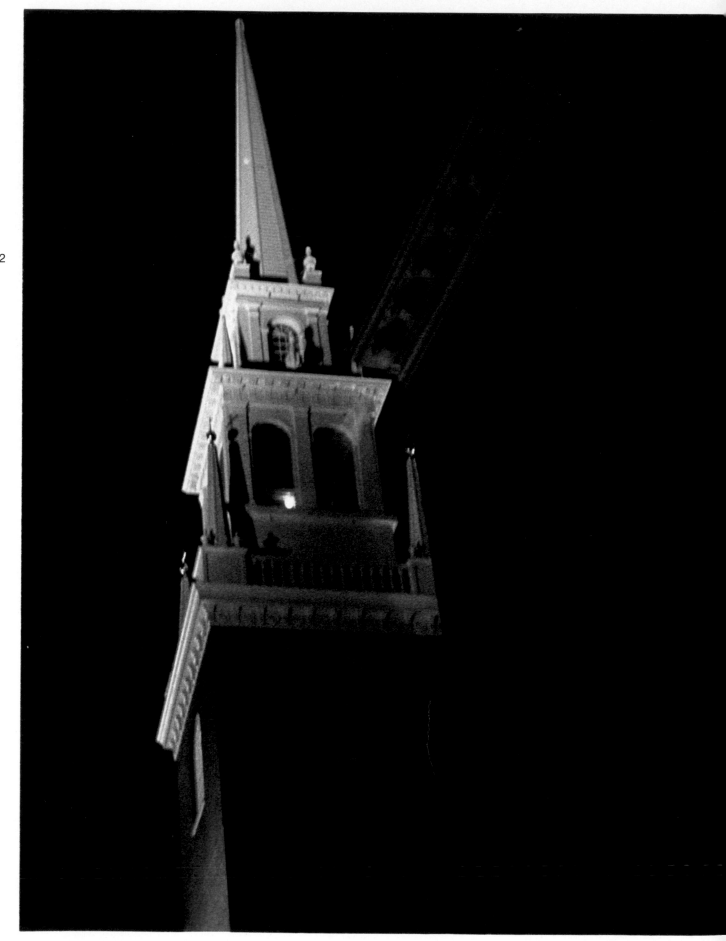

(opposite page) Old North Church, Boston

(bottom left) Third lantern lit by President Ford, assisted by Vicar Robert Golledge of Old North Church; (right top) lantern; (right bottom) lantern observed by former U.S. House Speaker John W. McCormack, ARBA Administrator John W. Warner and U.S. Senator Edward W. Brooke from Massachusetts

The Third Lantern

The stage was being set, on April 18, 1775, for history to be made. The express riders waited for the signal—one if by land, two if by sea. Would there be one lantern or two in the steeple of Old North Church?

Two hundred years later, at a reenactment of that eventful night, citizens of Boston watched President Ford light two lanterns like those that had started Paul Revere on his famous ride. Then later, they saw a third hoisted alongside the historic two. It symbolically lighted the way into our third century.

"The British Are Coming!"

The legendary midnight ride of Paul Revere on April 18, 1775, romanticized and immortalized by poet Henry Wadsworth Longfellow, has inspired generations of Americans. No matter that Revere was but one of several who spread the alarm as British troops marched out of Boston toward Concord. No matter that he was taken by the British before he ever reached Concord. The Boston silversmith, riding from village to village waking the sleeping colonists with the cry, "The British are coming!" has become a folk hero of the American Revolution.

A 61 year old retired contractor, Dino Di Carlo, saddled up at the Old North Church 200 years later to recreate the famous ride. The route had to be changed somewhat because the rolling meadows and quiet country lanes of Revere's day had given way to modern Boston's suburban sprawl. Our latter day Revere had to gallop through streets and over paved highways in order to spread the alarm from Boston to Lexington.

The sights he saw were quite different from those seen by his famous predecessor. Papa Gino's Pizzeria, Moriarity's Bar, Levine's Kosher Meat Market, the Wan Fu Chinese Restaurant—clearly, more than the terrain had changed during the 200 years since 13 English colonies began their fight for independence from the mother country!

Paul Revere rides again

The Shot Heard 'Round the World

On the morning of April 19, 1975, bells began ringing at 5:00 a.m. in Lexington and Concord, Massachusetts. Crowds huddled under umbrellas and parkas in the rainy predawn chill. On signal, Captain Jonas Parker, played by a 49 year old hairdresser, ordered his troop to "Stand!" on Lexington Green.

The British commanding officer (who had arrived with his company in three buses) cried, "Disperse, ye rebels!"

They refused, and battle was joined.

The realism of the 15 minute skirmish that followed was stunning. Flags waved in the breeze, old patriots wept, and children took in the scene with delight.

Later that day, President Ford addressed crowds totaling 160,000 at Lexington and Concord. In his speech at Concord, he called for "reconciliation and national unity."

His otherwise warm welcome was marred by jeers and shouts from some 5,000 protesters led by Jeremy Rifkin of the People's Bicentennial Commission. They provided a vivid reminder of the divisions and rancor remaining from the era of Vietnam and Watergate.

That same day at Lexington and Concord the troops refired "the shot heard 'round the world." That same evening it reverberated on television in millions of living rooms everywhere.

The Bicentennial had arrived!

Reenactment of Battles of Lexington and Concord, April 19, 1975

(opposite page, far right) Minuteman statue

History Lessons Abound

"Bicentennial" was becoming a household word. Besides reports of commemorative events on the evening news, television offered many special programs to audiences whose interest in our national heritage was growing constantly. *The Adams Chronicles, Suddenly—An Eagle,* Carl Sandburg's *Lincoln,* and the daily *Bicentennial Minutes* were among the host of offerings spread before viewers.

Americans did not have to travel great distances to find the Bicentennial. It was taking place in communities all across the country: the Battles of Lexington and Concord were fought once more—in Little Rock, Arkansas; Paul Revere rode again—in Flint, Michigan and Springfield, Illinois; the Old North Church lantern service was repeated—in Jackson, Mississippi. Millions more saw the Boston ceremony in a nationally distributed short film, *The Third Lantern For The Third Century,* produced by Boston's WBZ–TV and the ARBA's Office of Communications.

Battle of Bunker Hill reenactment, June 17, 1975

Bicentennial on the Road

For those who did travel to the places embedded in our memories as "where it all began," there were visitor attractions and hospitality in abundance. New York, Philadelphia, Boston and Washington, D.C. rolled out the red, white and blue carpets. The National Park Service created or improved visitor facilities at 20 major historic sites associated with the American Revolution. Exhibits ranging across much of our history—from the *America's Inventive Genius* exhibition in Chicago's Museum of Science and Industry to *USA '76: The First Two Hundred Years,* prepared by the ARBA—were shown in museums and other public places from coast to coast.

An exhibit of 500 documents, historical objects and models spanning our nation's 200 year history was displayed in 25 railroad cars pulled by a refurbished steam locomotive. The *American Freedom Train,* financed by American businesses, traveled to 137 cities in 48 states by the end of 1976 and was visited by millions.

The Freedom Train was not the only project to put the Bicentennial "on the road." The *Bicentennial Wagon Train Pilgrimage to Pennsylvania,* sponsored by the Pennsylvania Bicentennial Commission, kindled our imaginations by evoking memories of the hopes and bravery of pioneers making the long trek through the wilderness that was America.

The prairie schooners and Conestogas were gathered at Valley Forge State Park, Pennsylvania, on July 4, 1976—their final encampment and the end of a 17,000 mile journey that wound through 48 states.

The warm summer air and the park's neatly trimmed lawns provided a sharp contrast to the way it had been during the harsh winter of 1777, when General George Washington's ragged Continental Army bivouacked there in the snow. Victory for the Americans seemed an illusion during that dreadful winter. General Washington wrote: "you might have tracked the army from White Marsh to Valley Forge by the blood of their feet."

The faith and determination of the legendary Continental Army that won freedom for the fledgling nation, the imagination and endurance of the countless pioneers who set out on journeys that expanded the nation from 13 eastern seaboard colonies into 50 states spanning a continent and beyond—these were the qualities commemorated on Valley Forge's grassy knolls on July 4, 1976. The observance there was both solemn and festive. Two hundred years of remembered history evoked gratitude for the past and hope for the future.

(below) Armed Forces Bicentennial Exhibit Vans; *(right, top to bottom) Wagon Train, Lincoln Memorial, National Visitors Center (Washington, D.C.), Freedom Train*

Expeditions That Shaped History

The history of the United States is a history of ambition as well as achievement. The Bicentennial offered an opportunity to reexamine some of the daring and memorable journeys of our forebears.

The commemoration of Francisco Anastasio Dominguez and Francisco Silvestre Velez de Escalante recalled the expedition of those two Franciscan friars in 1776 through what is now the southwestern region of the United States. The reenactment in 1976 had both educational and cultural aspects rooted in the Spanish heritage of the region.

In 1681, Robert Cavelier Sieur de La Salle traveled by canoe from Canada to New Orleans and claimed the vast Mississippi watershed for the King of France. In September 1976, the *LaSalle: Expedition II*—six teachers, a playwright, a priest and 16 high school students, all dressed as 17th century pioneers—set out from Montreal in canoes to retrace La Salle's journey. The group paused along the way to give presentations recalling the French colonial era to schools and community groups.

The day of the riverboat was brought back to life at Ohio and Mississippi riverports visited by the sternwheelers *Delta Queen I* and *Delta Queen II*. Riverboat tours and concerts reminded people of the days when rivers were the main routes for travel and commerce in the central part of the nation. The shrill notes of a calliope, the blast of a steamboat whistle, the sight of a craft looking for all the world like a floating palace as it edged up to a public landing brought back an era immortalized by the pen of the great American novelist, Mark Twain.

Dominguez-Escalante expedition reenactment

(opposite page) Room in Independence Hall restored and refurnished as Bicentennial gift from the Daughters of the American Revolution

The Celebration's Common Thread

From beginning to end, one thread was to run through the Bicentennial planning. In his 1966 message to Congress recommending the creation of a Bicentennial commission, President Lyndon B. Johnson noted: "In the rich diversity that is America, each community will celebrate in its own way and will draw its own inspiration from the Revolution . . . The Bicentennial celebration should be a truly national effort."

One way the nation achieved this is visible in hundreds of communities, where preservation and restoration of historic buildings, landmarks and sites were part of local Bicentennial efforts.

The Grand Opera House in Wilmington, Delaware, built by Freemasons in 1871 to serve as their Grand Temple, now serves as the state's *Heritage '76* Meeting House.

The "Old Mission" at Cataldo, Idaho, built by members of the Coeur d'Alene Indian tribe between 1848 and 1853 under the supervision of a Jesuit missionary, has been restored and is now a state park.

Brickwork and windows of the First African Baptist Church in Savannah, Georgia have been restored. The church had been built by slaves before the Civil War.

The National Society of the Daughters of the American Revolution restored and refurnished two rooms at Independence Hall in Philadelphia as part of their Bicentennial contribution.

One of the most ambitious historic restoration efforts occurred in York, Pennsylvania. Inspired by a local attorney and history buff, John F. Rauhauser, Jr., the York County Bicentennial Commission reproduced, in full detail, the courthouse that was the meeting place for the Second Continental Congress when it was forced to flee Philadelphia in 1777. The Articles of Confederation, the first step toward national government, were drafted in York, Pennsylvania.

122 **Brick and Mortar Heritage**

Until recently, Americans, except for a hard core of dedicated preservationists, had seemed determined to get rid of old buildings and put modern ones in their places. The National Trust for Historic Preservation estimates that over the past 30 years more than a third of the structures declared to have historic or architectural significance were torn down.

During the Bicentennial, more Americans began to understand how important these structures were to their heritage and why they should be preserved. The National Register of Historic Places grew from fewer than 400 entries in 1969 to more than 13,000 in 1976.

Preservation costs money, and lack of funds often dooms historic structures to the wrecking ball. Beginning in 1973, the ARBC, and later the ARBA, provided more than $2 million to support state and local preservation efforts.

Meager funds were often augmented by volunteers skilled in carpentry, electrical work and other crafts. Those who could wield a paint brush or provide muscle power often made the crucial difference between restoration and demolition.

The citizens of Swanzey, New Hampshire preserved three historic bridges, two of which are now listed on the National Register of Historic Places. The volunteers did more than preserve the bridges for posterity. While working on them, they got to know each other better.

Even elementary school children got the restoration inspiration. In Bellevue, Washington, Spiritridge Elementary School students restored a neglected cemetery as their project.

(clockwise, beginning upper right) Frederick Douglass home, Washington, D.C.; Riverside, Wyoming; Boston, Massachusetts; Rock Creek Cemetery, Washington, D.C.

Restorations Planned

In May of 1973, the ARBC gave official recognition to the *Heritage '76 Meeting House Preservation Act,* begun by the National Trust for Historic Preservation and supported by the National Association of Home Builders. Each state, territory, the District of Columbia and the Commonwealth of Puerto Rico was encouraged to choose one site for preservation under the program, and a great many participated.

Other restoration projects abounded. Places ranged from an 18th century log cabin in Alaska to courthouses, grain mills, railroad stations and taverns—even to a casino in Puerto Rico and "Lucy"—the building shaped like an elephant in Atlantic City, New Jersey.

(counterclockwise, beginning upper left) Charleston, South Carolina; Carlyle House, Alexandria, Virginia; Court House, York, Pennsylvania; schoolhouse, Ada, Oklahoma

Local Projects Blossom

Exploration of the American heritage was not limited to brick and mortar projects. An extraordinary number of local histories were published, historical exhibits mounted, reenactments and pageants staged and tours of historic areas organized. Performances of American music, drama and dance abounded, leaving scarcely a corner of our cultural heritage neglected. From barbershop quartets in Kenosha, Wisconsin to a square dance festival in Anaheim, California, from concerts of colonial music in Edwardsville, Illinois to John Philip Sousa's comic operas in New York City and a jazz festival in Miami, Florida—the music of America's past delighted audiences from coast to coast.

Music, drama and dance

126 Washington Crossing Remembers

The *Bicentennial Communities Program* provided towns and villages with many ways to celebrate their heritage. The people of Bedford, a town of 16,000 in southern Indiana, had to obtain a specially constructed trailer and permission from four states to pass through with their extra-heavy load— their birthday gift to the nation. It is a 30 ton Indiana limestone sculpture depicting Washington crossing the Delaware. The Washington Crossing Foundation provided a site on the Pennsylvania side of the Delaware River, near where the general and his troops crossed the river on Christmas night to launch a surprise attack on Hessian mercenaries early on December 26, 1776.

Businesses and organizations in the Washington Crossing area joined with the foundation in providing the base on which the sculpture was mounted for its dedication on July 5, 1976.

Merle Edington, manager of the Bedford Chamber of Commerce, had conceived the idea as a Bicentennial gift to be enjoyed by Tricentennial visitors to the eastern cradles of liberty.

Gift from Bedford, Indiana to the nation, Washington Crossing, Pennsylvania

Above Ground Archaeology

In 1973, the ARBC defined "the heritage of America" as "the substance of our collective memory." By 1976, thanks in part to another ARBC program, it had become clear that it was, indeed, a massive collection.

In 1973, the ARBC issued a booklet with the intriguing title, *Above Ground Archaeology*. Written primarily for junior and senior high school students, the booklet showed ways to collect historic things around homes and communities. It inspired a kind of respect for the past and helped people discover what life was like in other times. Soon after the ARBA began operations in 1974, it printed an additional 30,000 copies of the booklet. They were sold through federal publications outlets—mostly to schools and youth groups across the nation.

The booklet triggered forays into basements and attics and trips to local libraries to unearth dusty maps and forgotten documents. Long-time residents were confronted with microphones and tape recorders and urged to remember aloud the "good old days."

This uncommon interest in our common heritage surely must have helped to swell the tidal wave of enthusiasm, pride and excitement that swept across the nation at the Bicentennial's peak on July 4, 1976.

Researching our history—in classrooms as well as outside—in many efforts to find tangible evidence of our past

The American experiment was—and still is—a magnet that has drawn immigrants from all over the world. This unique migration was what President Franklin D. Roosevelt had in mind when he addressed the Daughters of the American Revolution in 1938, saying "Remember, remember always that all of us, and you and I especially, are descended from immigrants and revolutionists."

Most of our ancestors came to these shores by boat. This helps explain why six million Americans lined the waterfront, peered from skyscraper windows and craned their necks from rooftops to see firsthand the tall ships glide majestically up the Hudson River past Manhattan on July 4, 1976.

Who could see this and not remember that in the distant or recent past, their ancestors had sailed across a sea to begin a new life in America?

No Hyphenated Americans

Greek-Americans from all over the country gathered at New York Harbor in March 1976 to climb aboard ferry boats bound for Liberty Island, there to join His Eminence, Archbishop Iakovos, Greek Orthodox Archbishop of North and South America, in paying tribute to America, a nation of nations and land of opportunity. "Is it any wonder that we say, 'God Bless America,' with such enthusiasm and devotion," read the invitation, "for while she has made us proud to be Americans, she has never once denied us the privilege of proclaiming our priceless Greek heritage."

In an address in 1915 to the Knights of Columbus, President Theodore Roosevelt had asserted, "There is no room in this country for hyphenated Americanism." Sixty years later, hyphens were still plentiful, and in the Bicentennial observance we rediscovered the remarkable assortment of ethnic backgrounds that have contributed to our national identity. Far from finding them submerged, we found the cultures that came together to build our country were still very much a part of the fabric of America today.

Our Ethnic Heritage

A quick look at the activities registered in the official Bicentennial Information Network proves that the contents of the "melting pot" have not yet melted. The bubbling pot was serving up a lavish feast of ethnic celebrations for the Bicentennial.

A dramatic bronze sculpture of "Young Meher," a legendary hero from Armenian folklore, was unveiled on Armenian Martyrs' Day in Philadelphia on April 24, 1976, a tribute to the Bicentennial from Armenian-Americans.

Napoleon Koscialkowski was the first person of Polish descent to settle in the Colorado Territory. He came in the mid-19th century. And Pauline Zabrinsky might be regarded as the state's prototype of today's feminist. She mined and prospected the Rockies. They and dozens of other Poles who followed their footsteps to Colorado and the Mile High City were the subject of an exhibit depicting the 120 year history of the Polish community in Denver.

In Hartford, Connecticut, 62 ethnic groups joined to document the diverse ethnic and racial communities in that city in a project called *Our Roots.*

Maryland and New Jersey published ethnic directories to emphasize the diversity of their communities and to provide information for foreign visitors.

In Detroit, Michigan and Charleston, South Carolina, and in other cities and towns, large and small, across the nation, millions took part in festivals proclaiming the cultural diversity of America. Irish and French, German and Czech, Polish and Italian, Finnish and Mexican, Chinese and Jewish, Latvian and Japanese—the music, costumes, crafts and foods of these and a hundred other cultures were savored as "American."

Many Voices, a film produced by the ARBA, tells it this way: "Together we make up America, strong and rich in its cultural variety, a vivid mosaic of our entire society, yet with each piece retaining its own bright and essential integrity."

A Legacy of Slavery

Not all the nation's immigrants boarded freely the ships that brought them here. Millions of Americans are descended from Africans who were transported here as articles of commerce—slaves—to labor at building America, with no hope of enjoying the rewards of freedom taken for granted by other Americans.

More than a century after the Civil War that had freed the slaves and offered them a thousand promises, many still unfulfilled, some Black Americans found little to celebrate as we approached our national anniversary. However, many Blacks did take part in the Bicentennial. Books, histories, films, exhibits and conferences explored the Black contribution to our national heritage. Special exhibits of the works of Black artists were held. Black music of the past was performed, along with new works by Black composers.

Historic figures and episodes in Black history, often left out of the standard history texts, were now being highlighted. Structures and sites associated with Black history were added to the National Register of Historic Places and, in many cases, restored—including, in Washington, D.C., the home of the famous abolitionist and orator, Frederick Douglass.

Thomas Cannon, a Black postal clerk in Richmond, Virginia, sent $50 to each of the 50 states as his personal birthday gift to the nation. In a letter accompanying the gifts, he wrote, "Her glaring inequities, racial prejudice, gross materialism and monumental egotism notwithstanding, America has been and still is the mightiest and most honorable among earthly nations, primarily because she is ensouled by a conscientious, generous and very compassionate people." True patriots, he said, "are those who seek to make America that which she is capable of becoming for the greater glory of God and man."

129

Black heritage—a search for roots

The Earliest Americans

Other Americans do not trace their beginnings on this continent to an ocean voyage. Forebears of the American Indian probably came on foot across the Bering Straits in a past so distant as to make our national history but the blink of an eye.

Many people believe the treatment of Native Americans as the nation spread west is an embarrassing blot on our national history. It came as no surprise, then, that Native Americans approached the Bicentennial observance with caution, coolness and, at times, bitterness. Why, after all, should the American Indian celebrate the founding of the nation which treated his ancestors to massacre and plunder, forcing them off the land occupied by his people for centuries? Charles Johnson, director of the Portland Urban Indian Program, declined an invitation to join a Bicentennial Wagon Train passing through Oregon. "We felt the invitation was like the Germans inviting the Jews to celebrate Hitler's rise to power," he said.

"Here Come the Beads and Trinkets!"

The ARBA was anxious to offer an opportunity for Native Americans to participate in the national observance, however. On January 30, 1975, John Warner met with representatives of 24 tribes to encourage them to see the Bicentennial as "a tremendous opportunity to awaken the entire nation to the richness of your heritage." Sitting in the conference room of the restored townhouse near the White House which served as the ARBA headquarters, Mr. Warner brought out a box of lapel pins depicting the national Bicentennial symbol. Watching from the other end of the large red felt-covered conference table, Doreen Bond, a Northern Cheyenne from Lame Deer, Montana, said, "Hooray! Here come the beads and trinkets." Undaunted, the administrator outlined the steps he had taken to provide assistance to Native American Bicentennial program efforts and predicted that, by 1976, American Indians would wear the lapel pins with pride.

Native Americans did wear the pins

and did take part in the Bicentennial observance, mounting impressive programs highlighting their traditions and culture, often with the assistance of funds provided by the ARBA.

Indians Favor Tangible Projects

The Seminole Nation of Oklahoma built a museum and library to house priceless objects which were part of the cultural history of their ancestors, together with written materials and recordings of the language, legends and folk tales of Seminole history.

Mid-America All Indian Center, Wichita, Kansas

Shoshones send welcoming party to South Pass, Wyoming

The Navajo Nation at Window Rock, Arizona completed a complex in which to display its heritage. It contains artifacts, films and exhibitions highlighting the native culture and traditions of the Navajo people.

Urban Indians are the special concern of the Mid-America All Indian Center in Wichita, Kansas. Early in 1974, the City of Wichita designated the center its primary Bicentennial project and committed land worth $1 million along with $2 million in construction and development funds. Dedicated on July 4, 1976, the center features a museum and library, a large multipurpose area called the Ceremonial Kiva and administrative offices. Visitors learn about Indian dwellings, the democratic government of America's first settlers, Indian poetry and foods. From career counseling and nutrition programs to powwows and classes in quilting, beading and leatherwork, the center will provide services to some 3,000 American Indians, members of 42 tribes in the Wichita area.

In Alaska, the Tlingit-Haida Council renovated a tribal and community house. The Anse Tribal Council carved two 30 foot totem poles.

As the Bicentennial celebration of Independence Day approached, John Warner said in an ARBA news release, "We are a nation of nations, proud of the richness and diversity of our cultures; the Bicentennial marks the end of any thought of being a melting pot."

Bicentennial America gave ample proof of the truth of this insight and gave us all a deeper appreciation of the national motto, E PLURIBUS UNUM.

Native Americans around the country celebrate the Bicentennial

Georgia Joins the Union

On September 5, 1974, Philadelphia Mayor Frank L. Rizzo and his wife welcomed governors and delegates from the states that had been the 13 original colonies to a breakfast in the courtyard of the restored home of Samuel Powel, Revolutionary mayor of the city. The breakfast preceded the opening of a two day commemoration of the First Continental Congress, hosted by Governor Milton J. Shapp.

Originally, delegates from 12 of the 13 colonies had met in Philadelphia to discuss their common grievances against George III. Georgia, the only state which chose not to take part in 1774, was represented in 1974 by then-Governor Jimmy Carter. Two years and four months later Governor Carter became President after winning a close election.

After the breakfast, the governors and delegates walked the few blocks from the Powel House to Carpenters' Hall, site of the first Congress, where the two day meeting was held.

The delegations had come to Philadelphia not just to celebrate the 200th anniversary of the Congress, but also to talk about their current problems in much the same way as their colonial predecessors. Like the first Congress, this assembly had no legislative authority, but that did not discourage enthusiasm as they debated the memorial resolutions introduced by Governor Shapp.

The old walls of Carpenters' Hall looked down once more on a group of delegates expressing public concern about the abuse of power and corruption of government. Less than a month before, the Watergate scandal, which had rocked the nation for more than a year, had come to a climax with the first resignation of a President.

Sobering as was this backdrop, it served to make the reason for the commemoration all that more compelling. The principles for which the colonists had fought and died, and the experiment in self-government that was based on those principles, had survived a severe and recent test.

At the closing banquet, held in a tent pitched in the shadow of Independence Hall, President Ford addressed the assembled members of Congress, state governors and delegates. The best way to commemorate the Bicentennial in 1976, he said, is for today's America to show the world "that the character and quality of the American people have not changed."

We Didn't Seek War

The delegates to the First Continental Congress were not of a mind to go to war with the mother country. They had come together to seek a redress of grievances. They could not know, in the fall of 1774, that their pleas would fall on deaf ears and that the ultimate solution would have to be war.

Having agreed on a statement of demands, they adjourned on October 26, 1774, intending to reconvene the following May only if they had not received satisfaction from the Crown. Certain that harmony would be restored, John Adams wrote in his diary as he left Philadelphia, "It is not likely that I shall ever see this part of the world again."

He was mistaken, of course. On May 10, 1775, Adams found himself far from home again in Philadelphia for the opening of the Second Continental Congress.

On May 10, 1975, Philadelphia '76 opened a six month commemoration of the Second Continental Congress.

Historic reenactments, ceremonies and city-wide festivities throughout the summer months of 1975 marked the 200th anniversary of the Congress whose deliberations ultimately led to the Declaration of Independence.

(below) Joint session of Congress to commemorate First Continental Congress, Washington, D.C.

(opposite page, bottom center) A new home for the Liberty Bell, Philadelphia, Pennsylvania; (middle right) the nation's governors assemble in Philadelphia, paying tribute to First Continental Congress; (middle center) President Ford opens Centennial Safe in the U.S. Capitol, Washington, D.C. Elsewhere across the nation—people celebrate in many ways

134 One Nation under God

Prayer was one of the first items of business to be discussed by the Congress in 1775. Benjamin Franklin argued convincingly that prayer should be an indispensable part of each day's proceedings—a custom which survives to this day in the Congress of the United States.

On June 12, 1775, the Congress unanimously passed a resolution setting aside July 20 as a day of prayer and fasting throughout the English colonies on this continent, "that these Colonies may be ever under the Care and Protection of a kind Providence" and that their "civil and religious Privileges may be secured to the latest Posterity: . . ."

On the designated day, members of the Second Continental Congress walked together from Independence Hall to Christ Church, four blocks away, where they heard a sermon preached by the Reverend Jacob Duche, rector of Christ Church and chaplain of the Congress. Upon their return, they were greeted with the welcome news that Georgia had joined the Congress, bringing to 13 the total number of rebelling colonies.

On June 12, 1975, recalling these events, President Ford proclaimed a national day of prayer to be observed in July as part of the Bicentennial. John W. Warner, commenting on this presidential proclamation, emphasized its significance. "We begin our third century of national life," he wrote in a report, *Religion and the Bicentennial*, "as we began our first—with a recognition of the importance of religious faith in the lives of millions of Americans."

Old North Church, Boston

Churches Join the Bicentennial

Early in our history as a nation, Alexis de Tocqueville, the French author, statesman and frequent visitor to America, wrote: "I sought the greatness of America in her harbors and commerce and mines and fertile fields, but it was not there. It was not until I entered her churches and found her pulpits aflame with righteousness that I understood the greatness of her power. America is great because America is good. And if she ever ceases to be good, she will cease to be great."

More than a century later, another distinguished visitor from abroad, Gilbert Keith Chesterton, the wry British author, called America a "nation with the soul of a church."

This identification with religion endures in America. According to 1976 figures, 131 million Americans belonged to 350,000 congregations. It is not surprising, then, that religion played an important part in the nation's Bicentennial observance.

Warner Expresses Hope

In May 1975, John Warner addressed a gathering of religious leaders drawn from more than 90 national denominations and organizations. He paid tribute to the essential role of religion in the life of the nation and expressed his hope that an equally significant contribution to the Bicentennial observance could be expected from the religious community.

He was not disappointed. In keeping with the ARBA's emphasis on popular participation, the national offices of religious organizations offered scores of new programs, suggestions and resource materials for use in local congregations. Individual churches and synagogues observed the national anniversary in a variety of ways—from worship services to lectures and discussion groups, potluck suppers and ice cream socials. Some of these events were specially designed for the Bicentennial; more often, perhaps, the Bicentennial had a way of creeping into the ordinary activities of a congregation. Members researched the history of their local church, studied religious freedom in America, took a hard look at the values of the nation, gave thanks for the blessings of the past, admitted the inability of the nation to live up altogether to the ideals embodied in our founding documents, but reaffirmed their commitment to achieve these ideals in the century to come.

(left, top) Touro Synagogue, Newport, Rhode Island

(left, center and bottom) The Mission of the Sacred Heart at Cataldo, restored as an Idaho Bicentennial Commission project

Not only in the churches were the ideals and values of the republic held up to scrutiny. Congress felt that, in planning for the Bicentennial, special emphasis should be given to the ideas associated with the Revolution which have been so important in the development of the United States in world affairs and in mankind's quest for freedom. Countless books, articles and radio and television programs explored the American heritage from every vantage point.

Conferences, lectures and symposia concentrated on the basic principles of American democracy and their application to the questions faced by America today. *The Bicentennial Conference on the U.S. Constitution, The Federalist Papers Reexamined, The Bicentennial Conference on Religious Liberty, The Nature of a Humane Society Bicentennial Symposium, National Bicentennial Consultation on Religion and the American Experience*— these are but a representative sampling of the national conferences officially recognized by the ARBA.

The American Catholic Church conferred with its members across the country during 1976

The *American Issues Forum*

Important as they were, most Americans did not attend conferences such as these. But this does not mean that Americans did not discuss the basic issues of our society. Lounging on a bench on Main Street, enjoying the "eleventh frame" at the local bowling alley, sitting around the family dinner table, sipping coffee during the morning office break or a beer at the corner tavern in the evening, Americans discussed and discussed the issues, and then discussed some more. We are, and always have been, a nation of talkers.

Walter Cronkite of CBS News suggested, at a meeting of the White House Fellows, that this enduring characteristic of the American people be made the basis of a major national Bicentennial effort. Why not a nationwide dialogue for the Bicentennial? A dialogue about our country—what it is, how it got that way, where it is headed?

The National Endowment for the Humanities and the ARBA took up the idea, and, under the auspices of the Endowment, a calendar of topics of perennial importance to American life was developed as the framework for a national conversation. The *American Issues Forum,* as it was called, was an agenda of nine topics, ranging from our land to our form of government and our national aspirations, to be discussed monthly from September 1975 through May 1976.

An impressive array of organizations joined to support this effort, providing forum-related materials from their own perspective and urging their constituents to take part. The American Library Association, the AFL–CIO, the National Association of Manufacturers, The Interchurch Center, The Adult Education Association of the U.S.A., the National Council on the Aging, the National Association for the Advancement of Colored People, The National Center for Urban Ethnic Affairs—the list goes on, resembling a "Who's Who" of associations who have supported the American tradition of voluntarism.

Copies of the American Issues Forum Calendar arrived in magazines and mailings, were printed in newspapers and newsletters, were found in local banks and public libraries. A wealth of material had been developed or gathered on forum topics. Formal and informal discussion groups took them up, though the extent of the nationwide dialogue within the forum framework cannot be measured, since no reporting procedure was made part of it. But Americans did converse during the Bicentennial, and the forum materials were widely disseminated.

Our 200 Years: Tradition and Renewal

American Issues Forum

A National Bicentennial Program

Summary Calendar and Film Discussion Guide

The American Issues Forum calendar of topics

Neither 1776 nor 1976 an End

As July 4, 1976 approached, the administrator was quoted in an ARBA news release: "The Bicentennial has been a great learning experience. Americans have added to their knowledge of history, particularly the significance of our blueprints of government—the Declaration of Independence, the Constitution and the Bill of Rights. . . ."

The year 1776 did not mark the end of the American Revolution, nor did 1976 mark the end of the Bicentennial. The events of the Revolution will continue to be marked by other ceremonies and reenactments and many more commemorative activities through the anniversaries of the Treaty of Paris in 1983 and the Constitutional Convention in 1987. And, in a broader sense, the American Revolution itself will continue as long as we "keep the republic" bequeathed us by the men and women whose deeds we are celebrating in the Bicentennial.

This national anniversary has given us a remarkable opportunity to look once again at our heritage. Our pride in the achievements of the past two centuries has been tempered by failures that are also a part of our history. We grumble and sometimes anguish over the problems we face as a nation today. And, like our forebears who gathered in Philadelphia two centuries ago, we are rarely unanimous in our opinions. But we are held together by our common commitment to the truths we still hold to be self-evident, as enunciated in the Declaration of Independence.

Benjamin Franklin would be pleased to see that we have been able to "keep the republic" he helped forge in his later years. If appreciation of our heritage has grown during the Bicentennial observance, this can only help us to grow still more during our third century.

A commemoration usually reveals as much about the present as it does about the past. The American Revolution Bicentennial was no exception. America took a good look at itself and saw a nation old enough to have "a past to remember," young enough to have "a future to mold."

139

Cyclorama showing the growth of America—Rapid City, South Dakota

(opposite page) Yorktown, Virginia

The Diversity of
Our Culture

Navajo, Crow, Blackfeet, Sioux and Cherokee danced and sang together, in full regalia, during the first all-Indian Bicentennial rodeo and powwow, November 3–6, 1976, at Salt Lake City, Utah. It was a celebration of Indian ways, Indian history, Indian cowboys and Indian future in the third century of American independence.

A few months earlier, in Kansas City, Missouri, German-Americans frolicked to the tunes of the 37 piece Stadtkapelle brass band from Mengen, Germany. Rounds of German food and beer were punctuated by shouts of "Gesundheit!"

Senior citizens taught Girl Scouts to quilt, darn, knit, make corn-husk dolls and candles as part of Craft Day in Quincy, Illinois.

(preceding pages) Boston's "federal plaza"

(clockwise, beginning upper right) American Indians, *Festival of American Folklife; quilting in Lexington, South Carolina; Pomeranian dancers from Germany; Native American potter*

(opposite page, clockwise, beginning top) Performing on the lawn at Kennedy Center; streets of Tabor, South Dakota; Honor America Day in the nation's capital; fiddlers at the Festival of American Folklife

144

Civilization Comes Slowly

In a letter to his wife, Abigail, in 1780, John Adams wrote, "I must study politics and war, that my sons may have liberty to study mathematics and philosophy, geography, natural history and naval architecture, navigation, commerce, and agriculture, in order to give their children a right to study painting, poetry, music, architecture, statuary, tapestry, and porcelain."

As the nation he helped found closed its second century, Adams' dream of the future seemed about to be realized.

America celebrated with a nationwide Bicentennial birthday party. Everyone in the nation was invited to take part. Other nations of the world were invited to join in. The rich cultural heritage of a young nation was everywhere in evidence. A kaleidoscope of music and dance, theater and poetry, painting, sculpture, architecture and folk crafts exploded across the nation with a brightness and diversity that rivaled the fireworks of the 4th of July.

(opposite page) Bicentennial concert at Springdale Amphitheatre, Utah

(top) Up With People musical troupe, Washington, D.C.; (bottom) Water and Sky Festival of the Bicentennial Horizons of American Music—BHAM program, St. Louis, Missouri

146

Festival USA

Festival USA was the name finally chosen by the American Revolution Bicentennial Commission (ARBC) for a Bicentennial theme embracing the fine arts and folk crafts, the international and domestic roots of America's different cultures and traditions and the warmth and hospitality regarded as a vital part of the American character.

Formerly called *Open House USA, Festival USA* was a theme broad enough to contain singing and dancing, parades and fireworks, sailing ships and band concerts, sculptural masterpieces and painted fireplugs. *Festival USA* was an invitation to dust off the family heirlooms, spruce up the family homestead—and celebrate.

Quincy, Illinois

The Sound of Festival Music

"The hills were alive with the sound of music"—as were the valleys and the plains of Bicentennial America. The music of America's past and present was heard across the land, a living record of a nation's joys and sorrows, triumphs and tragedies, hopes and aspirations. Music brought from other lands and music welling up from the American experience. Symphony orchestras and brass bands, dulcimers and banjos. The voices of barbershop quartets and church choirs. The magic of music gave life to the nation's celebration.

The entire city of St. Louis was turned into a gigantic stage for three weeks, from June 14 to July 4, 1976. *Bicentennial Horizons of American Music and Art* presented music and drama ranging from symphony concerts to theater productions and jazz and bluegrass performances. An outdoor midnight carnival turned the city buildings into a musical instrument. Thousands jammed the halls and auditoriums, the parks and plazas of St. Louis to experience the sights and sounds of the city's Bicentennial centerpiece.

Biloxi, Mississippi was the first stop in a six month Bicentennial tour by the American Wind Symphony Orchestra. Beginning on April 30, 1976, the orchestra, housed in a new Floating Arts Center, visited major ports along the inland waterways and the Atlantic Coast. Free concerts on the barge, along with performances and workshops in local schools, attracted thousands in the 76 cities visited by the 45 member orchestra. On September 3, the Floating Arts Center docked at its home port, Pittsburgh, to present its program of music, theater and dance.

America sings

148

Age and style were not a factor in Bicentennial music festivals which entertained millions of people, 1972 through 1976

(opposite page, upper left) Choir of the First Baptist Church and Marching 100 School Band of Belton, Texas; (lower left) Chapel Choir of the First Baptist Church in Dallas, Texas; (far right) people celebrating with music

150 Strike Up the Band

The J. C. Penney Company invited Americans across the nation to "strike up the band" for the Bicentennial. More than 54,000 boxes of music were distributed to over 30,000 schools, churches, choral societies, police and fire departments and public libraries. Arranged for bands, choruses and orchestras, this collection of music reflected 200 years of America's history.

Hundreds of letters poured into J. C. Penney headquarters expressing appreciation for the company's Bicentennial gift. From an Adrian, Michigan high school: "Your gift to the nation's school music groups . . . shows foresight, dedication and sensitivity . . . you have made a fine contribution to our nation's musical literature."

Elsewhere . . . more than 100 concert and marching bands from all over the world showed up in North Dakota for a competition spanning four weekends in July 1976. The International Youth Band Festival's musical salute to the Bicentennial was sponsored by the North Dakota Bicentennial commission, the International Peace Garden, the International Music Camp and the Turtle Mountain communities in North Dakota.

J. C. Penney's Band Kit (one of three musical kits)

(opposite page, left) July 4th, 1976 fireworks near Statue of Liberty, New York City; (right) Arthur Fiedler concert, Boston, Massachusetts

Musical Parade at Kennedy Center

During 1976, the National Music Council organized a *Bicentennial Parade of American Music* at the John F. Kennedy Center for the Performing Arts in the nation's capital, featuring performing groups from every state in the nation.

The Kennedy Center was also the place chosen by the Society for the Preservation and Encouragement of Barbershop Quartet Singing for the premier performance on January 31, 1976 of its Bicentennial show, *America Sings*. Script and music were distributed to the society's 600 chapters for their use during the Bicentennial year.

Square dance devotees took a look at the origin and development of this American art form during their annual convention in Anaheim, California in June of the Bicentennial year. The National Square Dance Convention encouraged square dancers to participate in "trail dances" as they made their way to Anaheim.

Irish-American musicians were sought out in Chicago, Cleveland, Philadelphia, New York and Boston to record their art. Guitar music in the old Hawaiian slack key style and songs of the Southern Arapaho Indians were recorded in Bicentennial projects funded by the National Endowment for the Arts.

And Musical Landmarks . . .

New compositions inspired by the Bicentennial were added to the American musical treasury. Florissant Valley Community College near St. Louis, Missouri saw the premier of *U. Sam & Co., An Historical New Musical,* written in honor of America's 200th anniversary. The Mormon Tabernacle Choir and the Utah Symphony Orchestra performed together for the first time to present *A New Morning, Symphony No. 4.* And from a De Kalb, Illinois composer came a 40 minute symphonic poem called *Jack and Jill at Bunker Hill,* which had its official debut in New Orleans in 1976.

In 1860, the famed American poet, Walt Whitman, wrote in *Leaves of Grass,* "I hear America singing, the varied carols I hear." More than a century later America was still singing as she celebrated her 200th anniversary. On July 4th, when the Bicentennial reached its peak, millions of voices were raised across the land in celebration. Arthur Fiedler and the Boston Pops played to an enthusiastic crowd in Boston, while millions who gathered at New York Harbor to see the Statue of Liberty aglow with fireworks joined their hearts and voices in the national anthem.

151

152

Many Took to the Road

The whole nation was on display during the Bicentennial, and many Americans took to the road to take in its delights.

(left top) Using new bike lanes; (left bottom) Lower Falls, Yellowstone National Park; (right bottom) Independence Hall Steeple

The Smith family—Maria and Paul, daughter Marlene and son Joe—leased their farm in Collins, Missouri and began a trip on July 4, 1975 that took them to all 50 states before they returned home a year later.

Working and traveling became a way of life for the Smiths, who started out with $500. They camped in an apricot orchard in Washington and lived in a "picker's cabin" in California's Salinas Valley, where they picked bell peppers and broccoli to raise enough money to fly to Hawaii. "One minute we're eating peanut butter sandwiches," Marlene reminisced, "and the next we're eating the specialty of the state in a fancy restaurant."

And there was 19 year old Dan Ambrose, who set out to walk in the footsteps of the Franciscan monks who founded California's mission system in the 1700's. Authentically attired in a rough wool habit and accompanied only by a burro named Holly, Dan strode out of the courtyard at Mission San Diego de la Alcala, determined to walk the entire length of the mission trail—all 900 miles of it. Dan's dream was to get a glimpse of what it took to carve a place in history, armed only with courage and faith.

Just Plain Tourists

For most travelers, more conventional modes of transportation were used to reach the historic sites that had a special appeal to Bicentennial visitors. Exhibits, performances and special tours were added to the usual attractions in many cities, especially those associated with the Revolution.

153

Tours and picnics: (clockwise, beginning upper left) Wisconsin, Washington, D.C., Utah, Connecticut

154 **Boston Starts Early**

History had led Boston to start early. The year 1973 marked the 200th anniversary of the famous Tea Party in Boston Harbor. The weekend commemoration of that event was a spectacular and diversified affair that attracted tens of thousands of visitors and residents. Boston's Bicentennial machinery was already in gear. Its creative and practical approach to providing visitor services and planning events and activities led the ARBA to fund special efforts in Boston as models for other communities.

Based on its experiences in planning the 200th anniversary commemoration of the Boston Tea Party in 1973, Boston 200, the city's official Bicentennial organization, produced an *Event Planning Workbook.* This publication covered every conceivable detail for planners and provided hints and checklists to make sure nothing was forgotten, including the clean-up detail.

Boston 200 next turned its talents to visitor services. A program, *City Host,* was developed to help those who were already providing hospitality to visitors. The City Hosts who signed up worked in hotels, restaurants, airport terminals, taxicabs, museums and historic sites in the Boston area. An orientation program gave them information on the latest Bicentennial events and other activities in the city and suggested ways to handle problems encountered by visitors. Another booklet, *City Host: A Program to Improve Visitor Services,* was distributed nationwide to share the experience of this model program with other communities.

Boston, Massachusetts, April 18, 1975

National Parks Go Bicentennial

Bicentennial visitors to the ever-popular national parks found special activities and events in abundance. The National Park Service had invested three years and $100 million in new and expanded visitor centers, dramas and historical vignettes, films, exhibits, publications and living history programs:

An ethnic festival at Gateway National Recreation Area in New York; 18th century magic, art and musical performances at Saratoga National Historical Park in New York; a celebration of mountain music at Cumberland Gap National Historical Park in Kentucky; a demonstration of Blackfeet Indian culture at Glacier National Park in Montana; a Fiesta of the Arts at Chamizal National Memorial in Texas. These and many other delights greeted visitors to the national parks from Colonial National Historical Park in Yorktown, Virginia to Haleakala National Park in Hawaii, as the National Park Service hosted a festival of America's cultural heritage for the national anniversary.

Yorktown, Virginia reenactment

156 **America on Parade**

Disneyland in California and Disney World in Florida focused on America's history and heroes as they prepared to entertain 25 million visitors during 1975 and 1976. Each of the 50 states, in the order of their entry into the union, received special attention for a week. Guest high school and college bands from every corner of the nation performed for the crowds who came to witness *America on Parade*.

In the Nation's Capital

Fireworks in the 18th century French style provided a flamboyant opening for *The Eye of Thomas Jefferson* exhibit in the nation's capital. Based on the life of Thomas Jefferson, the visual arts of his day and his own enthusiastic interest in them, this was the most complex exhibition ever mounted by the National Gallery of Art.

During the summer of 1976, visitors to Washington could choose from more than 40 major exhibits highlighting cultural influences from abroad as well as homegrown American cultural forms. *America as Art, America on Stage, Our Changing Land—Ecology 200* and *"We, the People"* were among the exhibits that offered a panorama of our 200 year American experience to those who traveled to the nation's capital.

158 On the Road

Small town America bustled with activity as it put out the welcome mat for visitors. "Everybody in [our] county is taking part," remarked Mrs. Jessie Walker, Bicentennial chairperson of Preston, Georgia. The ripsnorter of a celebration she organized in December 1975 featured patriotic speeches, handicrafts by artisans from around the state and such exotic delicacies as chitterling sandwiches and barbecued deer. Mayor Billy Rees, Sheriff George E. Goare and assorted citizens decorated the veterans' monument for the occasion. The three member police department even bought new uniforms, and people who didn't pitch in and work made donations.

Upwards of 20,000 people were expected in this little Webster County crossroads town (population 226) to see the *U.S. Armed Forces Bicentennial Exhibit Vans.*

Officially recognized as a federal agency program, this traveling exhibition of American military history was sponsored by the Department of Defense. Its appearance in many towns and cities across the nation sparked a flurry of activity similar to that of Preston's.

And in the Center Ring . . .

The Greatest Show on Earth went on the road in 1975 and 1976 decked out in red, white and blue. Millions of circus-goers viewed the Bicentennial salute presented by Ringling Brothers and Barnum and Bailey. A brief history of the circus in America was included as part of the printed program given to spectators in the 85 cities on the tour circuit. Two circus museums, one in Florida and the other in Wisconsin, also received a Bicentennial refurbishing, as had the circus acts.

Touring exhibits and performing groups moved across the country to delight the eyes and ears of millions of Americans. *Amistad II: Afro/American Touring Arts Program,* featuring Afro-American art work created between 1790 and 1975; *U.S.A. '76: The First Two Hundred Years,* prepared by the ARBA—these and a host of other "moveable feasts" helped put the Bicentennial on the road.

Smithsonian's Folklife Festival

The summer-long Smithsonian *Festival of American Folklife* of 1976 was a fitting climax to its previous 10 years of celebrating folk traditions, arts and skills of America. With these years of experience, coupled with the enthusiastic cooperation of 38 foreign governments, 42 unions and organizations, 117 Native American tribal groups and communities and individuals from every region of the country, a 12 week spectacular outdoor event was held in our nation's capital on the Mall between the Washington Monument and the Lincoln Memorial.

Americans in all parts of the country had an opportunity to share this Bicentennial project, as 700 of the folk singers, dancers and craftspeople from foreign countries followed their appearance in Washington with a three week nationwide tour by various groups. Throughout the summer, 116 performances were held in 61 cities in 30 states. They included performances by Liberian stilt dancers, Israeli wedding musicians, Scandinavian fiddlers, Brazilian capoeira dancers, Japanese wheel puppeteers and many other traditional performers.

Many faces at the Festival of American Folklife; *aerial view of Folklife Festival on the Mall, summer of '76 (opposite page, upper left)*

162　Local History—Quilted

Americans also celebrated their culture and traditions in their own backyards. From her sketches of landscapes and buildings in Mott, North Dakota, Mrs. Reinhardt Hirning created quilting squares that told a visual history of the tiny town at the turn of the century; the Senior Citizen Ladies Club of Hebron, North Dakota did the quilting. In Richmond, Virginia, a quarter of a million stitches, 550 yards of thread and 1,000 hours of sewing went into a quilt that captured 12 scenes in Virginia's history from 1607 to 1890. It was made by 22 women enrolled in a quilting course at the Virginia Commonwealth University Center for Continuing Education.

Twenty-seven women in the tiny village of Villanueva in northern New Mexico recounted their town's history in a 265 foot long tapestry made for the walls of their old church. The embroidery project told the history of this Spanish-American village and Our Lady of Guadalupe Church from the time before the land was inhabited to the present day.

Rediscovering Our Communities

Quincy, Illinois; Tacoma, Washington; and Galveston, Texas were chosen as model communities when the ARBA invited cities and towns across the nation to join *Community Rediscovery '76.* Within the pages of the accounts of community efforts, assembled over three months, are stories of how an empty downtown store was turned into a community exhibit center and the architecture of a town was inventoried.

There are reports of how school children prepared a child's eye view of the early history of one town, while railroad buffs helped rekindle interest in preserving part of another town's early industrial history.

Craftsmen, poets, merchants, prison inmates, newspapers, banks, senior citizens, school teachers and administrators, local industries, libraries and an Indian chief—all became involved in "rediscovering" their communities.

The results included exhibits of needlepoint, toys, local products, railroading, the work of local artists and the histories of life on the wharf, the farm and the river. There were festivals, preservation efforts, cookbooks, bibliographies, guidebooks, lectures, photography shows, special programs for Christmas, walking tours, slide shows, craft demonstrations and storytelling hours.

From Quincy, Illinois, this comment: "Buildings, faces and situations that appear commonplace by virtue of daily contact, are perceived by us with the intense curiosity of a traveler in a journey through an uncharted land."

(opposite page, clockwise, beginning upper left) Central City, Colorado; Boston, Massachusetts; Mystic, Connecticut; Washington, D.C.; Washington, D.C.; Washington, D.C.; Navajo flag weaving; (middle) Leland, Michigan

164 A Permanent Legacy

Modern sculpture was the focus of a major *Festival USA* program in Nebraska. Ten sculptors chosen by a national panel of art experts each designed a monumental outdoor sculpture to be placed at one of the various rest stops along Interstate 80, which crosses this midwestern state. Key cities along the route provided the artists-in-residence with places to live as they created works of art that would become a permanent legacy of the Bicentennial.

And for Spectators . . .

Football fans across the nation received a Bicentennial bonus on January 18, 1976 when they tuned into the televised annual National Football League championship game. The Superbowl X half-time show was dedicated to the Bicentennial. It was viewed by a television audience in excess of 70 million.

(right) Three of Nebraska's 10 outdoor sculptures on Interstate 80

Film fans, too, had their day. On June 27, 1976, the doors of the Kennedy Center's Opera House opened for the premiere showing of *America at the Movies.* Produced by the American Film Institute for the ARBA, this feature length film used scenes from 83 films as a celebration of that peculiarly American genius that has produced moments of emotion that transcend nation or ideology, history or current events— moments that touch the core of the human spirit and are timeless.

Television screens across the nation carried the invitation to celebrate to millions, as 1976 opened with the *Tournament of Roses Parade,* which had a Bicentennial theme.

This two hour floral extravaganza saluting the nation's 200th birthday comprised 60 flower-covered floats, 22 bands and more than 240 equestrian riders in the five and one-half mile pageant that is a New Year's Day tradition. Highlighting the parade was a special Bicentennial "prologue" including a colonial color guard and a Revolutionary War fife and drum corps.

Tournament of Roses Parade

Building Toward the Crescendo

As the Bicentennial year unfolded, the celebration built to a crescendo that peaked on the weekend of weekends, July 2 to 5—Bicentennial Weekend. Parades and fireworks, singing and dancing, pealing bells and steamboat whistles—the jubilant outbursts of a nation's festival provided a fitting climax to the celebration begun many months before in cities, towns and villages across the land.

The full panoply of American life and culture had been put on display. The panorama was stunning. The trivial and the profound, the ephemeral and the timeless in the American experience marched side by side in a grand parade that was *Festival USA.*

Americans celebrated—on stage, in parks, at town squares. They mingled the past and present to express joy and gratitude and hope—and in the process learned a bit more about themselves.

(upper left) 1976 U.S. National Hot Air Balloon Championship; (lower left) Around the World Auto Race

(opposite page, clockwise, beginning upper left) Washington, D.C.; Centennial, Wyoming; New York Harbor; Boston, Massachusetts; Warrenton, Virginia; Cupertino, California; San Antonio, Texas; Fort Scott, Kansas (middle)

Into the Third
Century

Horizons—
A Future to Mold

170

"Come up with a program that somebody will give a damn about in 50 years." The mayor of Salina, Kansas was challenging the city's Bicentennial committee to think beyond the inevitable fireworks, parades and picnics.

They did. On May 1, 1976, Salina's Outdoor Environmental Laboratory was dedicated—15 acres of undisturbed prairie and riverbank set aside for learning and enjoyment.

Salina's mayor was echoing a challenge heard in thousands of cities, towns and villages across the nation. Bicentennial projects as diverse as the nation itself were starting up throughout the country, aimed at improving the quality of life as we began our third century.

When President Lyndon B. Johnson asked Congress in 1966 to establish a commission to coordinate Bicentennial planning, the scope and nature of the observance were by no means self-evident. There were few models to study—the obvious one was the Centennial of 1876—and the new commission was left to its own devices.

Dunes in Indiana

A Centerpiece in 1876

In 1876 a massive exhibition, the centerpiece of the Centennial observance, had drawn millions to Philadelphia to view its wonders. Gadgets and machines of every kind, including a curious "talking-box" invented by Alexander Graham Bell, testified to the progress the young nation had made in its first century and reflected the optimism and national pride of the time. As the year 1876 had opened, the lead editorial of *The New York Herald* exuded confidence: "The last hundred years have been the most fruitful and the most glorious period of equal length in the history of the human race . . . We are entering a year which will be ever memorable in our annals and which the nation has made fitting preparations to celebrate."

A Different Time

Bicentennial America was quite different from Centennial America. Our technological and industrial growth exceeded even the wildest imaginings of awe-struck visitors at the Centennial International Exhibition.

Bicentennial planners were faced with the task of designing a national observance for a nation in which natural resources were no longer deemed infinite and industrial expansion was no longer viewed as an unmixed blessing. The technology which had brought unprecedented material prosperity had also contributed heavily to the destruction of the environment and unleashed weapons capable of devastation previously unimaginable. The nation, and indeed the whole earth, had grown smaller through explosive transportation and communications advances. "Progress" was now being measured by the quality of life.

By July 4, 1970, the American Revolution Bicentennial Commission (ARBC) had submitted its report to President Richard M. Nixon. It contained a framework for the celebration that it felt was appropriate to the occasion and that, at the same time, reflected the hopes and aspirations of Bicentennial America. While giving proper emphasis to persons, places and events of the past, as well as to the diverse cultural heritage of America, the ARBC recommended that all Americans become involved in at least one project which would manifest the pride, priorities and hopes of their communities.

In his message to Congress of September 1970, President Nixon enthusiastically endorsed this recommendation. "Improving the quality of life is, in a sense, a more compelling concept in this era of advanced technology than it was in the time of Jefferson. I believe that this is the area in which we will find the fundamental theme for our anniversary observance of the continuing revolution that is the United States of America."

Metro Center station, Washington, D.C.

172 Into the Third Century

This theme—called *Horizons '76*—broadened the meaning of the national observance. The Bicentennial was not only the end of America's first two centuries of national life. It was also a time to usher in the third century of the continuing American Revolution.

Horizons '76 provided a dynamic approach to the celebration, suggesting steady growth. At the same time, this theme had about it an inherent modesty. The horizon is, after all, only as far as the eye can see. It was a theme that could, and did, appeal to the American people. It challenged the people of every community to provide something of value that would remain after the red, white and blue bunting was taken down, the bands had gone home and the fireworks had burned out.

The challenge was broad enough to include a new public library in Casey County, Kentucky and the world's largest statue of a Canadian snow goose in Sumner, Missouri.

More than 7,940 *Horizons* projects were recorded in the computerized Bicentennial Information Network. And in fact, there are believed to be many more that were not formally registered. Altogether, they provide a picture of the concerns and values, the hopes and aspirations of Bicentennial America.

(upper right) Sumner, Missouri; (bottom left) Oklahoma; (bottom right) New York City

(opposite page, top) Arizona; (bottom) Utah

Voices Together

On Sunday, July 4, 1976, the strains of *America The Beautiful* echoed throughout the land. In churches, public parks and village squares, at the Washington Monument and the Statue of Liberty, Americans sang of "amber waves of grain," "purple mountain majesties" and "fruited plains." The sentiments of this popular hymn by the educator and author Katharine Lee Bates captured the American spirit so faithfully that the song has become something of a second, unofficial national anthem by popular acclaim.

The bountiful, seemingly limitless land had beckoned the early settlers and provided food, clothing, shelter and energy for a young nation on the move.

And part of the American dream has always been to own a piece of that land. There seemed to be plenty to go around. The 20th century American poet, Gertrude Stein, reflected this attitude when she wrote, "In the United States there is more space where nobody is than where anybody is. This is what makes America what it is."

Saving the American Dream

As America approached its 200th birthday, however, the warnings of President Theodore Roosevelt and other early conservationists could no longer be taken lightly. Americans were reading in newspapers and hearing on radio and television disturbing stories of air and water pollution and dwindling natural resources. No longer could the expansive countryside and natural forests be taken for granted. Oil and gasoline prices soared, and the federal government pleaded with the people to conserve fuel for the winter ahead as the nation faced the energy crisis of 1973–74.

As America peeked over the threshold to the third century, the natural heritage she held so dear—the land—seemed to be slipping away.

Bicentennial America's horizon included projects designed to preserve this natural heritage for herself and for future generations.

174

Planting for Posterity

In December 1974, Bicentennial Administrator John W. Warner suggested that one gift every American could give Uncle Sam was a tree, plant or shrub—a living Bicentennial gift, a pleasant beginning for the third century. At the time, he was presenting a Bicentennial flag to the American Association of Nurserymen in recognition of their Green Survival program. The nurserymen had developed a series of steps that could be taken by the average person to improve the environment by planting and landscaping. They pledged to support the Bicentennial through an effort to bring these recommendations to the public.

Planting trees—in backyards, in public parks and along riverbanks—became a popular Bicentennial activity everywhere. Volunteers in Kent, Washington planted more than 2,000 trees to restore the greenery along the Green River. In Aberdeen, Maryland, government agencies, local clubs, businesses and individuals joined forces to beautify Route 22 with the addition of 1,776 trees. The people of Greeley, Colorado can now stroll through a botanical garden that is a product of their community Bicentennial effort. In Fallon, Nevada, the Bicentennial commission sponsored a city park, named in honor of Laura Mills, a well-loved teacher who had spent her entire adult life teaching children in the county school. One resident remarked, "There is hardly a person who was not taught by Laura Mills."

The Izaak Walton League of America issued a Bicentennial SOS, a call for help to save waterways and streams from pollution. During 1976, the League's Water Wagon logged more than 40,000 miles spreading a clean water message: *Save Our Streams— Adopt One.*

Students who participated in Ohio's *Watershed Heritage Project,* sponsored by the Institute for Environmental Education in Cleveland, learned to monitor water quality and other environmental factors. A seventh grade student said, "It makes you realize that where you live is important."

Two centuries ago, most of the three billion acres that are now the United States were in their natural state. But as the nation grew, they were cleared, leveled, dug up, paved over and built on, acre after acre. America's natural heritage was rapidly diminishing after 200 years.

The ARBA encouraged efforts to preserve this natural heritage for future generations. Official recognition was given to The Nature Conservancy for its program to acquire and preserve thousands of acres of scenic natural areas. Turtle Island off the coast of South Carolina, Willa Cather Prairie in Nebraska, Eagle Refuge in Washington and Hemlock Bluffs, Indiana—all are part of the Bicentennial legacy of the Land '76 program.

In communities like Lynchburg, Virginia; Urbana, Illinois; and Fairfield, Connecticut, the Bicentennial meant preserving Blackwater Creek, Boneyard Creek and the Sturges Wildlife Park.

(lower right) Mrs. Lyndon B. Johnson at dedication of Lyndon Baines Johnson Memorial Grove on the Potomac, *Washington, D.C.*

176   **Side by Side**

Along with America's astounding technological progress came a shorter work week. People living in cities and suburbs who were concerned about enhancing the quality of community life recognized the need for more opportunities to enjoy their leisure.

Pleasant places for people to gather and do things together were the answer. Thousands of parks were created for the Bicentennial.

Community organizations in Snohomish, Washington converted a quarter mile stretch of city riverfront into a public park for recreation at no cost to the city. The people and government of Fort Lauderdale, Florida developed a quiet park in the city's downtown district as their Bicentennial project.

In May 1976, the Spanish Land Grant Park in Florissant, Missouri was dedicated to the pioneers of Florissant Valley. The town's Bicentennial committee organized the financial and volunteer efforts for the park, which had originally been a gift to the township of St. Ferdinand from the King of Spain in 1788. Its purchase and restoration brought together diverse civic groups, the city and the county in a common project.

Since the mid-17th century, the South Street Seaport in New York City has been an active maritime trading center. The Bicentennial saw a new kind of activity in progress in this waterfront area of lower Manhattan. Present and future generations will now be able to enjoy the cultural and historical park that was created as the heart of a new residential complex expected to house more than 100,000 people by 1980. Museums, archives, renovated historic buildings and shops, films, theater, musical performances and exhibits of arts and crafts give both residents and visitors a better appreciation of the maritime history and culture of the city.

(left) Boston, Massachusetts; (right, top and bottom) New York City

Taming the Wilderness

When John Hancock and his colleagues in the Second Continental Congress signed the Declaration of Independence in 1776, only five percent of the population of the new United States lived in cities. Thomas Jefferson had always hoped that the new republic would remain largely agricultural and rural.

His hope was not realized. The wilderness was tamed. The Industrial Revolution, which followed the American Revolution, brought immigrants by the millions, seeking a new life in cities where, some believed, the streets were paved with gold. As America approached its 200th birthday, 70 percent of the people lived in cities and their suburbs.

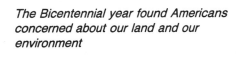

The Bicentennial year found Americans concerned about our land and our environment

Taming the Cities

In 1976, Americans stepped boldly into the next century with projects that revealed some of their hopes and dreams for their cities in the years ahead.

Downtown Cincinnati, Ohio was in the midst of an urban face-lift. Old buildings were being renovated and new ones built, sidewalks widened and trees planted. Over the years a nightmare of unaesthetic traffic signals and stop signs, telephone booths and trash cans, had littered the streets. *Operation Streetscape* replaced them with street furniture that was pleasing to look at and more efficient. This Bicentennial project helped make the center city a more pleasant place to work, shop and live.

"We have started a quiet revolution." The Junior League of Bergen County, New Jersey was referring to its participation in a national program begun by the Committees for Resource Recovery. Mayors in many urban areas have said that their number one problem is "what to do with the garbage." The Resource Recovery program reclaims old newspapers, recovers non-paper materials and eventually will recycle waste to make fuel, steam and fertilizer.

Johnny on the Spot

Johnny Horizon, with his ranger hat and outdoors look, became a familiar figure on the urban scene, too, as America prepared for its big birthday. The Department of the Interior received 60,000 requests for information about this Bicentennial program each month, most from city dwellers. Johnny appeared on bumper stickers, trash cans and litter bags, urging us to "clean up America for our 200th birthday." Adults and children aplenty signed on to clean up their neighborhoods, schools, parks and streets.

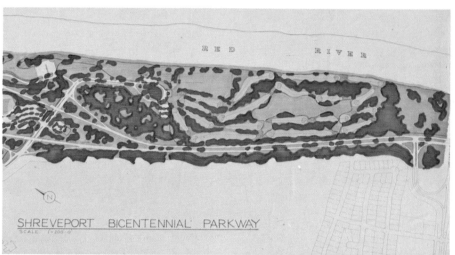

SHREVEPORT BICENTENNIAL PARKWAY
SCALE 1"=200'-0"

A Patchwork of Neighborhoods

The living cells of the city are its neighborhoods. Not always easy to define, the boundaries of one neighborhood often seem to melt into those of the next. Their picturesque names often reflect a past remembered only by old-timers and devotees of local history. Mount Auburn, Belmont, Lockerbie Square, College View, Pleasant Ridge, Hillwood Manor, Over-the-Rhine—houses and streets, churches and schools, parks and vacant lots—these are the places where people live, work, play, shop and worship. These are the pieces that make up our cities. In many cities, these

neighborhoods were the focus of Bicentennial horizons.

Maintenance of vacant lots is no longer a problem in Syracuse, New York. So many residents responded to the Bicentennial call to *Adopt-a-Lot* that there were not enough to go around. Using donated gardening supplies,

families and groups transformed vacant city lots into gardens—a welcome transformation in any neighborhood!

In San Antonio, Texas, the Alamo Plaza, site of Mexican General Antonio López de Santa Anna's legendary siege, was redeveloped as a "people place." A visitors' center, a bandstand, places to

sit and a bit of history made the plaza so attractive that owners of buildings in the surrounding area began a face-lift of their own.

The streets of the cities may not be paved with gold. But projects like these and thousands more did leave them aglow with life and hope for the future.

180

Horizons on Display

Many of the projects undertaken by urban and rural communities were able to draw on successful examples of local problem-solving highlighted through another major Bicentennial program—*Horizons on Display.*

As we entered the Bicentennial year, it was clear that the quality of life in many of our communities was being threatened by a host of social and economic problems. Throughout the nation, however, solutions were being found to cope with some of these seemingly insurmountable situations. Concern for these major problems—and recognition of the many grassroots efforts that were working—led to this *Horizons '76* program. *Horizons on Display* provided one more way for people to participate in the Bicentennial.

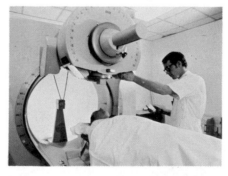

The Department of Housing and Urban Development and the ARBA believed that these efforts could, collectively, be the basis of a unique program spotlighting innovative problem-solving programs that could significantly improve the quality of life at the community level.

Horizons on Display was developed to encourage the sharing of these experiences with other communities and gave dramatic and further visible proof that the nation was the exposition for the Bicentennial.

Under *Horizons on Display*, recognition was given to 200 examples of community projects that were addressing problems in the fields of citizen involvement, communications, community development, economic development, the environment, health, human values and understanding, learning, leisure and transportation.

A fitting tribute was bestowed on the *Horizons on Display* program when it was chosen as the official American demonstration program for *Habitat*, the United Nations conference on human settlements, held in Canada in 1976.

(top left) Model of Colorado State Judicial Heritage Center; (top right) model of Streets for People program, Washington, D.C.; (middle left) new construction in nation's capital; (middle right) Denver, Colorado

(opposite page, top) John W. Warner and Mrs. Lindy Boggs at press conference; (middle left) Horizons on Display *symbol; (across bottom, left to right) ARBA officially recognized programs:* Committees for Resource Recovery; International Syncon; Horizons on Display

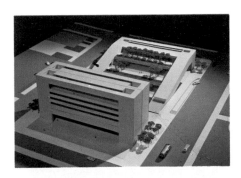

Concern for America's People

182

President James A. Garfield once wrote, "Territory is but the body of a nation. The people who inhabit its hills and valleys are its soul, its spirit, its life." America is people—young and old, rich and poor, blue collar and white collar, people whose ancestors came from every race and nation on earth.

The Bicentennial featured them all.

Independence for Our Elderly

A declining birth rate, coupled with longer life expectancy, have assured a larger proportion of older Americans in the years ahead. Offering the wisdom and experience that come only with age, senior citizen groups around the nation played an active role in Bicentennial projects.

The National Council on the Aging, however, was especially concerned about the more than one million older Americans confined to their homes and the millions of others facing conditions that threaten their independence.

Operation Independence was the council's response. Endorsed by the ARBA, this program sought to unite private and public agencies to deliver services to older persons in their homes so that they could continue to lead independent lives and take a full part in the life of the community.

In the Chinatown-North Beach area of San Francisco, a day health care center serves more than 100 elderly Chinese, Filipino and Italian-Americans. A Bicentennial effort, the On Lok Senior Health Services is the difference between independent living and institutionalization for these older Americans.

Future Homemakers of America working with senior citizens

Services, Services, Services

Health service delivery for the young as well as the old became a priority in many Bicentennial communities. The people of Hartford, Wisconsin were asked by their Bicentennial committee to submit ideas for projects they would like to see accomplished for the Bicentennial in their community.

The number one choice of the people in this town of 6,500 was the establishment of an emergency medical services unit. Now heart attack victims, trapped children and victims of home and street accidents are among the emergencies to which the new volunteer emergency squad responds.

Mrs. Betty L. Bumpers, wife of the then-governor of Arkansas, started a successful *Horizons '76* effort in her state to increase the number of children immunized against disease, thereby averting the threat of serious epidemics. So successful was the *Every Child in '74* immunization campaign that Mrs. Bumpers took it to the nation as *Every Child in '76/'77,* enlisting the aid of the National League for Nursing. Other national voluntary organizations and corporations also joined this effort in preventive medicine for the nation's third century.

Services to meet a variety of human needs and to improve life in the years ahead emerged in many communities. Fort Worth, Texas established a Parenting Guidance Center to help parents and parents-to-be with the problems, anxieties and adjustments involved in raising children. This center is now a permanent addition to the services offered in the community.

Women seeking to enter or reenter the job market in San Jose, California were the focus of that community's Bicentennial *Horizons '76* effort.

OUTREACH for Women offers resume writing, career counseling and job information and placement services "as a Bicentennial commemoration to the achievements of women in our society."

The 900 people of Hooper, Nebraska enjoy the benefits of a new public library as they step into the third century. An old building in the business district, donated to the town for this purpose, was completely renovated, mostly by volunteers. The enthusiasm and dedication of the townspeople will be tapped again to turn additional space in the building into a Hooper Museum.

Teens Who Care, a group of young people in Louisville, Kentucky, organized over 50 clubs throughout the state to increase public awareness of and support for the mentally handicapped. One club refurbished an old railroad caboose for use as a playroom for the special education class of a local mental health center.

Future Homemakers of America improving our social and physical environment through participation in BICEP—Bicentennial Environmental Program

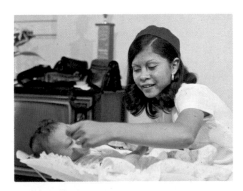

Graffiti Becomes Respectable

184

People who have to look at graffiti generally regard it as an expensive nuisance—crass, unsightly, offensive. That was pretty much the attitude at Estrada Court, a 414 unit Housing Authority development in East Los Angeles, California in the heart of the city's Mexican-American community. Residents very much wanted to be rid of the crude renderings of bored Estrada teenagers, for whom traditional recreational programs held no appeal.

The Bicentennial offered a chance for the nontraditional and resulted in a solution that made everybody happy.

The teenagers sought the assistance of an artist, formerly of the complex, for their own Bicentennial project. The artist agreed, the authority provided paint and approval, the Fire Department gave the scaffolding.

With all that, the teenagers covered three walls with more than 70 beautiful murals, many featuring patriotic, ethnic and cultural scenes.

The teenagers have reason to be proud of their creations, which residents can be sure won't be defaced. The murals are so popular they have been used in the opening and closing footage of the National Broadcasting Company's weekly television series, *Chico and the Man.*

Estrada Court in East Los Angeles, California

Tomorrow's Legacy

Bicentennial America's efforts to look to the horizon and do something of worth for tomorrow is a striking confirmation of American poet Archibald MacLeish's insight into the spirit of the nation, "America is promises."

The first words of the United States Constitution are, "We the People." Bicentennial America looked to her horizons and, in projects great and small, "We the People" still came first.

This emphasis on participation by all Americans was a main thrust of the ARBA's leadership during the final years of shaping the national celebration.

The ARBA not only endorsed worthy future-oriented programs, but it also invested some of its own limited funds in support of model programs with long-range potential.

Americans heard the Bicentennial *Call for Achievement* in 1976, inviting them to establish ways for citizens to become involved in setting priorities and seeking solutions to problems in their own community. They were invited to read, hear and see the success stories of other communities which had answered the call.

For example, people in nine Maryland suburbs of the nation's capital, distressed by a decline in community services, formed the Neighborhoods Uniting Project. By working together, residents of these "forgotten" communities were able to reverse the trend. Attitudes were changed—those of local government officials as well as residents—and services were restored or increased.

Another example offered to those who responded to the call was the 13 year struggle of an old inner-city neighborhood in Hartford, Connecticut. Having escaped the bulldozers of urban renewal, the South Arsenal neighborhood revitalized itself. New housing and a new school designed by the residents themselves are part of the story.

The larger and more complex a society grows, the more people who want to do something about their problems experience frustration. Where do they go to find help?

Ten model Community Resource Centers were established across the nation to provide information about community services and public policies and ways to encourage dialogue and cooperative action. A "how-to" manual funded by the ARBA helps other communities build on these models.

The impact of the program? There are now over 60 centers around the country, and more on the way.

The Near and Distant Future

Americans were concerned about the near future as well as the long-range future during the Bicentennial.

As Junction City, Kansas approached the Bicentennial, this town of 19,000 had an opportunity to do more than talk. Unlike many towns and cities, Junction City was about to pay off its bond issues and needed to decide how to use future revenues to best advantage. Junction City used the Bicentennial as an opportunity to set priorities and act on them. By July 1976, they were ready to enter the third century proudly—with a new medical clinic, new park land, new fire trucks, a downtown face-lift and a host of other improvements.

In Georgia, Governor George D. Busbee hosted a Youth Congress to consider the future of the state and the nation. For three days in February of the Bicentennial year, 150 young delegates looked to that future, guided by advisors from universities and city governments throughout the state. Sponsors believed that the *Declaration of the Future* adopted by the Youth Congress "has caused many to recognize the need for planning for the future."

In Leesburg, Virginia, 30 miles from the nation's capital, a series of three day forums were sponsored by the National Science Foundation, the Xerox Corporation and the ARBA to explore "knowledge" in the next quarter century. The 350 participants, drawn from a variety of disciplines and backgrounds, discussed the generation, transmission and uses of knowledge. The goal of *Knowledge 2000* was to make possible better public decisions on America's future.

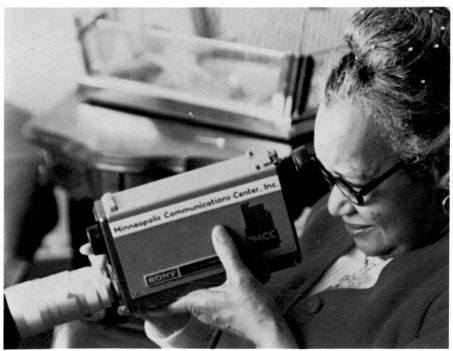

One Way to a Better Future

America's traditional concern with education was reflected in community improvement efforts for the third century. The National Education Association developed *Declaration of Interdependence: Education for a Global Community*—its effort to play an active part in changing the future course of American education by embracing the ideas of a global community, equality and interdependence of all peoples and nations, and education as a tool to bring about world peace.

According to another *Horizons* educational project, *Reading Is Fun-damental,* despite the nation's historic commitment to universal education, 21 million Americans could not read the Declaration of Independence in 1976.

Reading Is Fun-damental addressed this problem by stimulating interest in reading and providing books for children in inner cities, in barrios, on Indian reservations, in Appalachia's hollows and in poor rural areas—one more effort to serve people and improve the nation as America passed the 200 year mark.

A young woman from Guttenberg, New Jersey will remember the Bicentennial as the beginning of her path to a nursing career. She was the first to benefit from a scholarship fund established by the people of this town of 5,700 as a living memorial to the Bicentennial.

(top) Dial-A-Bus, Rochester, New York; (bottom) Model Cities Communications Center, Minneapolis, Minnesota

Looking to the Tricentennial

Americans did look ahead during the Bicentennial, but not to all that distant a future. They could foresee the Tricentennial with no greater clarity than Centennial Americans could have foreseen 1976. But they did look to the horizon—as far as their eyes could see. They wanted to do something of value for the occasion. And what they did—in cities, towns and villages across the nation—reflected the America they loved: the land, the cities, the people.

History may not record the Bicentennial as a giant step into the future. But Bicentennial America hopes that Americans of 2076 will look back with pride on their ancestors who stepped boldly and confidently into the century they will close.

Blue Birds in Oklahoma plant trees for Century III

People,
People,
People

Participants Not Spectators— A Special Emphasis

"The success of the Bicentennial will be judged by the number of participants, not spectators."

This observation by John W. Warner rather precisely outlined the challenge he faced when Vice President Gerald R. Ford swore him in as Bicentennial administrator on April 11, 1974. Standing on the steps of the Capitol, Warner promised the Vice President that the newly-created American Revolution Bicentennial Administration (ARBA) would make an all-out effort to encourage the maximum number of Americans to participate actively in their Bicentennial.

By the end of 1976, it was generally apparent that this test had been passed with flying colors. Americans, individually and collectively, had indeed participated. Other chapters in this book illustrate well the who and how of this participation. This chapter discusses areas of special concern to the ARBA and its predecessor, the American Revolution Bicentennial Commission (ARBC), in carrying out their assignments to stimulate interest and participation in the commemoration of the nation's 200th anniversary.

People celebrate: (preceding pages) in Boston, April 1975; (this page, opposite page) around the country

Seeking Total Involvement

As the nation reached the maturity that comes with the experience of 200 years, Americans became more and more aware that rather than being a "melting pot," they were a pluralistic society built on diverse ethnic and racial contributions, cultures and heritages. The celebration of this diversity became an important part of the Bicentennial.

Within that concept, the ARBA encouraged and supported the involvement of all groups in the commemoration.

However, many Native Americans and Blacks were seriously questioning whether they had anything to celebrate. And three other segments of American society presented a different dilemma. Youth, women and ethnic groups let it be known emphatically that they wanted in and that they wanted a voice in shaping and forming the Bicentennial.

The Nation Ought to Know

Many Native Americans approached the Bicentennial with little enthusiasm. The American Indian Movement and other activist groups even suggested a counter-commemoration to celebrate the 100th anniversary of the Indian victory over General George A. Custer at the Battle of the Little Big Horn on June 25, 1876, or a boycott of the whole Bicentennial.

Others, however, recognized that the Bicentennial offered a way to show their pride in their heritage as the first Americans, call attention to their problems and work to build a better future.

At the prodding of Thomasine Hill, a Crow Indian and one of the newest and youngest members of the ARBC, a three day conference was held in Tucson, Arizona in January 1973 to explore the problem.

Rather than rejecting the idea of participation, 150 representatives of more than 30 Indian tribes in 20 states expressed strong interest in activities whose goals were to preserve their cultural identity, to promote a better understanding of American Indian customs and traditions and to improve the quality of their lives.

On July 1, 1974, the ARBA opened a Native American Programs Office in Denver, Colorado. Headed by a Blackfeet Indian, the office staff worked to bridge the gap between the Indian and non-Indian worlds.

Over $6 million in Title X funds from the Economic Development Administration in the U.S. Department of Commerce were funneled through the office to support Bicentennial projects that could reduce the high unemployment on reservations and at the same time begin much needed improvements. For instance, the Shoshone tribe in Wyoming used funds to launch a water and sewer project. Employment was provided for community members of the Standing Rock Sioux tribe through its renovation of historical sites on its reservation in North Dakota.

Because of his determination to involve Native Americans in the Bicentennial, Mr. Warner visited 111 different tribes, encouraging them to take part in the Bicentennial however they saw fit, but in any event to participate.

Many Native Americans responded. Thirty-eight tribes became official Bicentennial Communities in recognition of their efforts.

Native Americans show and tell of their cultural heritage; (lower left) Statue, Keeper of the Plains, Mid-America All Indian Center, Wichita, Kansas

194 Frederick Douglass Recalled

Many Blacks saw little to commemorate in the Bicentennial. During the late '60s and early '70s, some were echoing the words of Frederick Douglass, the outspoken Black leader who lived during the mid-19th century. In an address given in 1852 in Rochester, New York, Douglass viewed celebration of July 4th by Blacks in this manner: "This Fourth [of] July is yours, not mine. . . . What to the American slave, is your 4th of July? I answer; a day that reveals to him, more than all other days in the year, the gross injustice and cruelty to which he is the constant victim. To him, your celebration is a sham; . . ."

Fortunately, in the 1960's and '70s there were others who felt differently. Vincent A. deForest established the Afro-American Bicentennial Corporation (ABC) in December 1970 because: "Most important, we believe, is the special stake Black Americans have in communicating a more truthful interpretation of history in an attempt to clarify our rich heritage. Our [ABC's] plan would accentuate and accelerate this effort by Blacks in the years leading up to the Bicentennial anniversary."

With funds provided under a contract with the National Park Service, the ABC identified historic sites associated with the contributions of Blacks to the development of the United States. Where only three Black sites had been designated on the National Register of Historic Places before this effort, about 60 now appear.

Tributes to Blacks

Hurray for Black Women, a series of one day programs held in four midwestern cities in late 1976, for which the ARBA provided funds, involved a cross section of Black women. Developed by Madelyne Blunt and Associates in cooperation with the Association for the Study of Afro-American Life and History, the program paid tribute to the contributions of Black women to the nation, provided a forum for an exchange of ideas on how to improve the future and stimulated greater understanding and awareness.

Senator Edward W. Brooke (R-Mass), the nation's only Black U.S. Senator, was chairman of the ARB Board and vice-chairman of the congressional Joint Committee on Arrangements for the Commemoration of the Bicentennial. He was instrumental in the publication of a booklet on the 45 Black Americans who have served in the Congress.

Under the ARBA's matching grant program, over a half million dollars went through state Bicentennial commissions to 156 programs involving Blacks.

(right top) Get out the vote program; (right lower) citizen involvement

(opposite page, top) Typical high school assembly program; (lower left) National Portrait Gallery exhibit, Washington, D.C.; (right) oral history and community clean-ups, Washington, D.C.

Ethnic, Racial Groups Meet

A milestone on the road to broader participation was reached on June 27, 1974 when the ARBA, in cooperation with James O. Gibson, chairman of the Bicentennial commission of the District of Columbia, and Monsignor Geno Baroni, director of the National Center for Urban Ethnic Affairs, sponsored a meeting in Washington, D.C.

More than 75 participants speaking for a cross section of national and community organizations came together to decide mutual priorities and to begin developing plans for the Bicentennial. This meeting marked the first time any federal agency had sought consultation with a broadly representative, culturally diverse ethnic and racial group.

In far-ranging discussions, the group outlined their major concerns, which included recognition of their ethnic and racial contributions to the building of America; the need to preserve and develop ethnic and community arts, music and folkways; the task of providing means of expression for diverse communities; and the need to provide a base for neighborhood restoration, preservation and economic development projects.

With needed support promised by the ARBA, the Bicentennial Ethnic/Racial Coalition (BERC), as the group titled itself, proceeded with arrangements for a much larger, more inclusive meeting, to be held in January 1975. This time, amid plentiful give-and-take, all viewpoints were covered by the more than 400 representatives of ethnic and racial groups from around the nation meeting in Washington, D.C.

Hispanic, Black, Pacific Islander, Middle Eastern, Asian, European, Native American and other groups caucused individually as ethnic units and then, in an effort to identify common objectives and goals, together with their peers in a "caucus of the caucuses." Conference delegates, working with federal and private sector officials, hammered out their problems in workshops addressing policies, priorities and needs with regard to Bicentennial programs.

In a further effort to stimulate diverse participation, on June 30 the ARBA announced the formation of an alliance of ethnic and racial organizations from around the nation to develop programs and activities for the Bicentennial. Sixty-nine organizations joined the alliance. They ranged from the Polish Union of America and the Japanese American Citizens League to the Frederick Douglass Institute, Museum of African Art, and the Italian Historical Society of America.

Administrator Gets Advice

In August 1975, several members of BERC's executive committee, along with other representatives of ethnic and racial communities, accepted appointment as a formal advisory committee to the administrator of the ARBA. This action followed months of trying to get funding as an independent nonprofit organization. Under the chairmanship of Dr. John A. Kromkowski, a professor of political science at the University of Notre Dame, the committee was instrumental in getting the ARB Board to adopt stronger guidelines encouraging states to give special consideration to projects related to racial and ethnic groups, women and youth.

From the beginning, all matching grant money provided to the states by the ARBA had been disbursed subject to these terms. Stronger emphasis on Black and minority groups followed the Board's action.

Warner Applauds Participation

In an assessment of the Bicentennial as he was leaving office, Mr. Warner put it this way: "Naturally, I am sorry that some of our people chose not to take part because of past wrongs. But I am proud and pleased to report that a great many Blacks and Native Americans did participate in substance and spirit. As a result, we all have gained a better understanding and appreciation for each other."

And as the Bicentennial year drew to a close, it was clear that literally thousands of programs throughout the states and communities had emphasized the great ethnic contributions to arts, crafts, music, festivals and culture in general, from border to border and coast to coast.

(opposite page) Participants at Bicentennial Ethnic/Racial Coalition (BERC) Conference

Participants at Bicentennial
Ethnic/Racial Coalition (BERC)
Conference headed by Monsignor Geno
Baroni and James O. Gibson

200 You'd Better Not Forget Us

Youth and women, as groups, also had special problems and concerns in connection with the Bicentennial commemoration. With both groups, it was not a question of participating. That they fully intended to do. Their concern was that they would be left out of the planning, that they would be ignored.

Young People Speak Bluntly

The Bicentennial commissioners discovered, on two heated occasions in 1971, that not all segments of America's young people were happy with the commemoration as it was then being planned.

A gathering of one group of youth took place in September 1971 at the Belmont Conference House in Elkridge, Maryland at the invitation of John D. Rockefeller, III, who had expressed concern about the need for bringing more young people into the celebration.

Twenty-two participants came from all parts of the country—from Alaska to Maine, California to Connecticut. The only things they had in common were their youth and their activist credentials. Later many of them attended an ARBC meeting in Chicago on October 8, 1971. On both occasions, their viewpoints were blunt and clear.

At the Belmont gathering, Bob Boyd, a young Black executive with Chrysler Corporation, summed up their feelings when he said: "All that people here are saying is that when it goes off, let's see to it that it's more than a great big birthday party."

In Chicago, the young people accused the ARBC, as then structured, of reflecting the values and ideas of a dominant culture. They said it did not speak for the many people who are not white, not male; people who do not have money; and people who are not educated. They suggested that if the Bicentennial were to be something worthwhile, these ignored groups had to be included.

It was an awkward beginning, but by early 1972 the ARBC had been expanded to include eight more public members, of whom four were representatives of youth. Of the eight, one was the head of the National Urban League, a national Black organization; one was a distinguished judge from Delaware; another was a Black law student; and the fourth, from Pennsylvania, was a member of the National Executive Board of the Boy Scouts of America. Two young women were chosen, one an Indian and pre-law student from Arizona, the other a member of the 1971 White House Conference on Youth. From the southwest, a Mexican-American educator was chosen, as was an internationally famous Black country and western musician. These new commissioners became active in working to secure participation of youth and minorities.

Young people create interest in Bicentennial through photographing local events and participating in school activities

School and youth organizations play
major Bicentennial roles

202

Youth and Education Efforts

Shortly after the ARBA replaced the ARBC in 1974, a Youth and Education Office was set up. Volunteer interns helped the staff in nationwide efforts to provide information about Bicentennial events and projects and to encourage participation in them. They even persuaded the popular singer, John Denver, to donate his time and talent (with the ARBA funding the production costs) to make two public service film spots to be used on television to encourage people—especially youth—to become involved in the celebration.

The ARBC earlier had recognized and funded intern programs that provided monies for young people so that they could assist regional Bicentennial planners.

(left top) Craft demonstration at Expo '74 *in Spokane, Washington; (left bottom and opposite page, top) Future Farmers of America and 4-H members from Michigan, Vermont, Louisiana and Oregon in a service program in western Honduras; (bottom) star of Future Homemakers of America in Mesa, Arizona*

U.S. Postal Service Delivers

The ARBA, along with the U.S. Postal Service and the National Association of Elementary School Principals, sponsored the *Junior Committees of Correspondence* program. Classroom learning kits urged elementary and junior high school students to follow the example of their revolutionary forebears by exchanging letters with each other. More than 20 million of the nation's youngsters used the kits and took part in the program.

The National Student Advisory Committee on Vocational Education sponsored a program designed to involve members of six vocational student organizations in projects to improve the environment. This effort received national recognition. Called *BICEP—Bicentennial Environmental Program,* it included the Distributive Education Clubs of America, the Future Business Leaders of America/Phi Beta Lambda, the Future Farmers of America, the Future Homemakers of America, the Office Education Association and the Vocational Industrial Clubs of America.

The ARBA also gave national recognition to Bicentennial activities of various other youth organizations, including the Boy and Girl Scouts, the Camp Fire Girls, the Speech Communication Association and the Hugh O'Brian Youth Foundation.

In short, there is every indication of widespread participation in the Bicentennial by the nation's young people. History should record that they did participate—with excitement, will and vigor.

204 **"Remember the Ladies"**

As the Founding Fathers were evolving and drafting the Declaration of Independence in Philadelphia in 1776, John Adams was admonished in a letter from his wife, Abigail, to "remember the ladies." Bicentennial planners were also admonished to "remember the ladies" by the following:

"RESOLVED THAT: The national women's organizations, meeting in Washington, D.C., on December 7, 1973, at the invitation of the American Revolution Bicentennial Commission recommend:

"(1) That the Administrator or Deputy Administrator of the newly created American Revolution Bicentennial Administration be a woman, and

"(2) That fifty percent (50%) of the ARB Advisory Council be women, with due consideration for minority representation, and

"(3) That at least four of the eleven members of the American Revolution Bicentennial Board be women, and that these appointed women be:

"(a) At least one from the House of Representatives,

"(b) Either the Chairman or Vice Chairman of the ARBA Council,

"(c) One or two from officers or staffs of the state Bicentennial commissions or comparable state bodies."

Boston, Massachusetts, 1973

This strongly worded resolution, unanimously adopted by the representatives of over 50 national women's organizations, served notice on President Richard M. Nixon and the future ARBA administrator that women expected to be included in Bicentennial planning to a greater extent than they had during the life of the ARBC.

This group of women convened even though the end of the ARBC was imminent. The timing was perfect. The effective date of the establishment of the ARBA was just over a month away.

Abigail Would Have Been Pleased

The message was received. Four women did serve on the ARB Board, the agency's policymaking body. One of them, U.S. Representative Lindy (Mrs. Hale) Boggs (D-La) also chaired the congressional Joint Committee on Arrangements for the Commemoration of the Bicentennial. The ARB Advisory Council had nine women members. Twenty-four state Bicentennial commissions had women as leaders at one time or another.

Women chaired four of the House subcommittees that had oversight responsibilities in various areas of ARBA operations; they further brought the women's point of view to Bicentennial planning. The Representatives were Julia Butler Hansen (D-Wash), Bella S. Abzug (D-NY), Patricia Schroeder (D-Colo) and Leonor K. Sullivan (D-Mo).

Women members of Congress were also largely responsible for a Bicentennial display in the Capitol—an exhibit featuring all the women who have served in Congress.

The deputy administrators of the ARBA were also women. Marjorie W. Lynch, the first appointee, left the ARBA to become Under Secretary of the Department of Health, Education and Welfare. Jean McKee, her successor, became acting administrator when John Warner resigned.

205

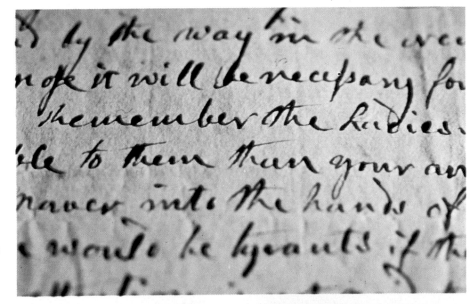

(top) Jean McKee, ARBA acting administrator; (middle) letter from Abigail Adams to husband, John Adams; (lower left) Marjorie W. Lynch, ARBA deputy administrator; (lower right) signing the Declaration of Independence, Philadelphia, September 4, 1974

Programs Emphasizing Women

In addition to settling the matter of women's representation, three national programs emphasizing women were approved at ARBC's winter 1973 meeting in Washington, D.C. They were: a *National Women's History/Resource Data Bank, Community Resource Centers* and an international women's arts festival. The first two programs were well underway at the close of the Bicentennial year in 1976, supported and funded by the ARBA. The third, the international women's arts festival, never materialized for lack of a financial sponsor. On the other hand, more than 60 sites around the nation became operational under the *Community Resource Centers* effort.

At national, regional, state and local levels, women not only participated in their nation's Bicentennial, but were active in all phases of planning it. And they were visible—something not always true during the course of the history they were celebrating.

In the summer of 1976, the ARBA issued a report on the Bicentennial achievements of women, sketching the variety and scope of their contributions to the success of the commemoration. In a foreword, Jean McKee, then deputy administrator, said:

"The women of this nation are participating in the Bicentennial as they have in so many projects which call for the volunteer who donates hard work, time and imagination.

"The American Revolution Bicentennial Administration feels it is important that the work of these women not pass by unnoticed as has so often

happened in the past. . . . let us as a nation resolve never again to ignore the contributions of any group. Our diversity gives us strength and reaffirms our fundamental freedoms."

One of the most significant of the Bicentennial projects relating to women was an exhibit assembled by the Pilgrim Society of Plymouth, Massachusetts. It examined the role of women in the Revolutionary War era—in warfare, commerce, education and religion. First opened in Plymouth, Massachusetts in June 1976, it was still traveling throughout the United States as this Bicentennial report was being printed. Appropriately, it is titled, *Remember the Ladies.*

Women took charge of many Bicentennial projects

Charges of Commercialism

The charge of commercializing the Bicentennial was another area of concern to the ARBC and the ARBA, particularly since the media had come up with "Buy-Centennial" as a catchword. There was a deep concern that this negative implication would overshadow the excellent efforts of the Bicentennial which were being sponsored by federal, state and local groups.

Some organizations objected to the business community's taking part in the commemoration in any way at all. The ARBA's position was that business not only had a right but a responsibility to participate to the fullest extent possible, though in dignified and appropriate ways. Administrator Warner pointed out over and over that this nation is based on a free enterprise system. Further, he maintained, history shows that far more immigrants came to this country to live as part of a free enterprise system than for any other reason, including escape from religious or other persecution.

On April 26, 1976, speaking to the Detroit Economic Club, he reported that the private sector was supporting over half the Bicentennial activities taking place across the country and should be proud of its efforts, regardless of the commercialism issue.

Involving Business

Special efforts were made to involve the business community in appropriate activities. One important part of the effort was to establish a private sector division in the ARBA whose main purpose was to interest corporations and businesses in supporting significant Bicentennial projects and programs.

National recognition was given to several corporate-sponsored endeavors, including Walt Disney Productions for their *America on Parade* and other entertaining and educational spectacles at Disney World and Disneyland. These were probably seen in person by more people than any other single Bicentennial attraction. Ringling Brothers and Barnum & Bailey Circus was also recognized for its Bicentennial version of The Greatest Show on Earth, its museums, and a history of the circus in America.

In addition, the ARBA established a business alliance to provide recognition and encouragement for company and employee Bicentennial efforts. Thirty-seven business organizations, including the Braniff International Corporation, EXXON Corporation and Marriott Corporation, were recognized.

America's private sector supported Bicentennial theater exhibits, museums, art and restorations

We're a Nation of Joiners

In early 1975, while the *Bicentennial Communities Program* was blossoming and other efforts were beginning to bear fruit, it became obvious that additional efforts were needed. The simple fact is that Americans are joiners and tend to think of themselves and to act as members of organizations, churches and so on.

Involving the many organizations with nationwide membership became a new objective. Since such groups had the potential for reaching millions of persons, two additional alliances were established to cover a variety of interests.

The National Bicentennial Service Alliance grew to be the largest, with 93 members. It included a variety of organizations ranging from The United States Jaycees and The American Legion to the American Trucking Associations, Inc. and B'nai B'rith/B'nai B'rith Women.

To encourage international participation in the Bicentennial, an alliance for host-type organizations was the next to be formed. The National Bicentennial Hospitality Alliance had 11 members, including People-to-People

International, Meridian House International and Friendship Ambassadors, Inc.

The National Bicentennial Sports Alliance included such groups as the Amateur Athletic Union, the American Bowling Congress, the Amateur Softball Association, Little League/Baseball, Inc. and the National Collegiate Athletic Association (NCAA). All told, 47 of the nation's major sports organizations joined.

In one way or another, more and more people participated. "Admittedly," Mr. Warner said in his final assessment, "the Bicentennial failed to meet the level of expectations of some—those who viewed it as a signal to push ahead with major needed social reform, or those who wished for spectacles tenfold greater than man's walking on the moon.

"But to the majority, it rekindled the 'can do' spirit that has been the fiber and strength of this nation throughout its 200 years. The Bicentennial generated the most massive volunteer effort in the history of peacetime America."

(opposite page, this page) ARBA developed alliances with service, business, sport and labor organizations

Foreign Countries
Take Part

214   Future generations may wonder why the international community joined so readily and enthusiastically in the Bicentennial of the United States of America. A comment by the Australian Bicentennial coordinator provides an answer: "We have a right to help you celebrate your Bicentennial, as 1775–1776 was a watershed in human development from which Canada, Australia, and many other countries benefitted and without which they could not have gained their independence."

Another reason for taking part was voiced by German television panel host Werner Hoefer: "My America is a colored man who—when I was a boy—gave me a piece of chocolate after World War One; an American who—when I became a man—gave a piece of chocolate to my children; an American who gave me the world edition of *The New York Times* under a POW tent in France; some movies of an Englishman named Charlie Chaplin; a bit of the Basin Street Blues, some lines from *Requiem for a Nun* by William Faulkner, and a chapter from *The Old Man and the Sea* by Ernest Hemingway. . . ."

A record of what is best described as official or quasi-official participation by foreign nations is published elsewhere in this report and provides an impressive listing.

(preceding pages) Sound and Light Spectacle at Mount Vernon: gift from the people of France

Invitation to the World, *July 4, 1972*

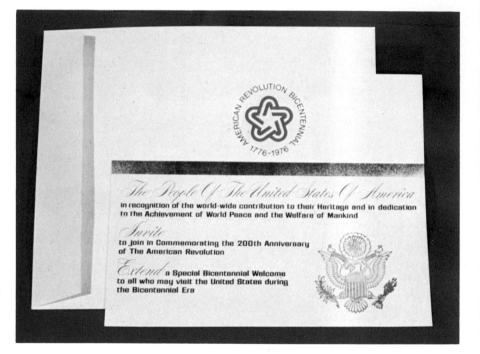

102 Joined Us

Official activities, coupled with countless efforts by individuals and private organizations in the United States and abroad, tell a Bicentennial story of international efforts as diverse as that of America's grassroots celebration itself. In many ways, it was extraordinary.

It is a story both grand and intimate, of friendship and concern, and of the significance to the world of the new form of government brought forth by the Declaration of Independence 200 years ago.

One hundred and two nations formally joined us in honoring America on its 200th anniversary. They represented every corner of the world:

Andorra, Argentina, Australia, Austria, Bahamas, Bahrain, Bangladesh, Barbados, Belgium, Benin, Bhutan, Bolivia, Brazil, Burundi, Cameroon, Canada, Chad, Chile, Republic of China, Colombia, Comoros, Costa Rica, Cyprus, Czechoslovakia, Denmark, Dominican Republic, Ecuador, Egypt, El Salvador, Equatorial Guinea, Finland, France, Gabon, The Gambia, Federal Republic of Germany,

Ghana, Greece, Grenada, Guatemala, Haiti, Hungary, Iceland, India, Indonesia, Iran, Ireland, Israel, Italy, Jamaica, Japan, Jordan, Korea, Lebanon, Liberia,

Luxembourg, Madagascar, Malaysia, Maldives, Mali, Mauritania, Mexico, Monaco, Morocco, Nepal, Netherlands, New Zealand, Nicaragua, Niger, Nigeria, Norway, Pakistan, Panama, Paraguay, Peru, Philippines, Poland, Portugal, Romania, Rwanda, Senegal, The Seychelles, Spain, Sri Lanka, Surinam, Swaziland, Sweden, Switzerland, Thailand, Togo, Tonga, Trinidad and Tobago, Tunisia, Turkey, Union of Soviet Socialist Republics, United Arab Emirates, United Kingdom, Upper Volta, Uruguay, Venezuela, Western Samoa, Yugoslavia, Zaire.

Foreign participation in the celebration was so diverse, so widespread and so interwoven with the Bicentennial tapestry that it made the celebration truly world-wide.

216 When John W. Warner was named administrator of the American Revolution Bicentennial Administration (ARBA) in April 1974, he predicted that a fourth of the Bicentennial would take place in the international arena.

His prophecy was borne out.

The diversity of participation was enormous—royal visits to the United States, groups of performing artists and touring exhibits, cultural exchanges and multinational festivals, issuance of commemorative stamps—each nation celebrated in a way significant and unique.

Some nations with close historical ties to the United States and the American Revolution came to the party like doting grandparents who had helped us grow up, happy for us, sharing national memories and hopes for the future.

Other nations, whose sons and daughters were the immigrants who built this country, came like parents to see how their children were doing and to help them rediscover their heritage.

Many nations came because the grand experiment in democracy, at age 200, is still a hope around the world.

Still others came out of courtesy,

some did not come at all, and some celebrated at home.

(below) Canadians from Kingston, Ontario march in Salute to Nations parade in Philadelphia, Pennsylvania

(opposite page, top left) Royal Winnepeg Ballet; (below left) experimental theater under construction in the John F. Kennedy Center, Washington, D.C., to be completed with a Bicentennial gift of $3 million from Japan; (top and bottom right) international visitors

218

Visiting foreign leaders: (left) King Juan Carlos of Spain; (opposite page, left) H.M. Queen Margrethe II and H.R.H. Prince Henrik of Denmark; and other international visitors

No Hard Feelings

For future readers, it should be said right now that the British seemed to enjoy the celebration almost as much as we Americans. And they provided two of the most exciting and memorable events of the occasion: a visit to the United States by Her Majesty, Queen Elizabeth II, direct descendant of the king who had aroused the wrath of the colonists; and the loan of one of the oldest known copies of the Magna Carta, for display in the United States Capitol during the Bicentennial year.

As one British writer put it, tongue in cheek: "After all, if we hadn't been so unreasonable, you wouldn't be what you are today."

Queen Elizabeth II visits the United States, July 1976

(opposite page) Magna Carta presentation ceremony, United States Capitol, Washington, D.C.

222 Une Alliance Historique

Not unexpectedly, our time-honored ally, France, played a major role. His Excellency Jacques Kosciusko-Morizet, French Ambassador to the United States, explained when he outlined his nation's program in January 1976:

"It's not hard to understand why we French have a special interest in this celebration since it marks not only the two hundred years of independence of the United States but also the two hundred years of friendship between France and America. There's never been a time when the United States has not been our friend and ally. At no time have our two countries been at war with each other. What is more, France played a part in the War of Independence and twice in this century Americans gave their lives for our liberation; this is something that the French people will never forget."

The itinerary of French President Valéry Giscard d'Estaing and his wife during their state visit to the United States from May 17 through 21, 1976, in honor of the Bicentennial, suggests the extent of French interest and commitment.

President Giscard d'Estaing presented France's official Bicentennial gift to the United States, a sound and light spectacle called *The Father of Liberty*. With George Washington's home at Mount Vernon for a backdrop, the show recalls the life of our first President, how he and the young Marquis de Lafayette met and how the friendship of the United States and France was born.

Later President Giscard d'Estaing took part in commemorative ceremonies at Yorktown, Virginia, where a French fleet tipped the scales in the decisive battle of the Revolutionary War; in

Philadelphia, where France's first representatives to Congress were accredited; in Houston, Texas, in honor of France's becoming the first foreign power to recognize Texas when it proclaimed its independence in 1836; and in New Orleans, where France's role in the development of the New World was remembered.

(left) Frenchmen show their colors; (right) visiting French citizens bring urn of earth from birthplace of Lafayette

Other French officials took part in commemorations at Valley Forge, Pennsylvania, where Lafayette spent the winter of 1778 with Washington; at Hull, Massachusetts, at the entrance to the Bay of Boston, where French Admiral Charles Hector d'Estaing anchored in the fall of 1778; in Savannah, Georgia, where the first joint French-American operations took place; at Newport, Rhode Island, where Ternay's fleet landed the French expeditionary corps under Comte de Rochambeau. There were also commemorations at Hartford, Connecticut, where the first historic meeting between Rochambeau and Washington took place; at Hartsdale, New York, where the French and American armies met and drew up plans for the Virginia campaign; at Virginia Beach, Virginia, where a British fleet was routed; and at Annapolis, Maryland, where in 1784 Congress ratified the Treaty of Paris.

In addition to marking historical moments in the relations of the two nations, France sent an array of cultural and art exhibits and performing groups, to the delight of American audiences.

(right) French musician entertains his American host

What to Wear?

Most international events occurred during the years 1975 and 1976. The pulling and hauling and shaping of the American commemoration had much to do with the manner and way in which foreign nations took part.

From the very beginning, foreign nations had indicated their desire to participate in the Bicentennial commemoration.

In retrospect, however, our foreign friends were in much the same situation as the person who doesn't know what to wear when first invited to a party. Dress for the occasion, indeed—the occasion itself had not been defined when the invitation was first sent.

Public Law 89–491 of July 4, 1966, which was signed by President Lyndon B. Johnson and created the American Revolution Bicentennial Commission (ARBC), read in part: ". . . it is appropriate and desirable to provide for the observation and commemoration of this anniversary and the events through local, State, National, and international activities. . . ." Public Law 93–179, which was enacted December 11, 1973 and established the ARBA, contained virtually the same language.

It was not until 1972, however, that the manner in which the Bicentennial would be commemorated was fully apparent—that it would be everywhere. There was to be no single international exposition.

To Have or Not to Have . . .

Understandably, foreign governments had been hesitant up to this point to think in terms of nationwide participation at a local level as long as there was a possibility there would be a major international exhibition in Philadelphia.

In a message to Congress on September 11, 1970, President Richard M. Nixon declared: "We should actively encourage international paticipation in our celebration. To do this in an orderly and well-planned way, we should select a principal site on which that international participation can focus." He then indicated his choice of Philadelphia over Boston, Miami and Washington, D.C. as the site for a Bicentennial exposition. On January 11, 1971, the choice was sanctioned by the Bureau of International Expositions.

The idea, of course, was that an exposition would provide an opportunity for other nations to display their achievements, talents, products and interests, thus providing an incentive for involvement in the Bicentennial.

There were many, however, who felt that a single site exposition might, for a variety of reasons, run counter to the concept of a nationwide Bicentennial.

Senator Edward W. Brooke (R–Mass), a member of the American Revolution Bicentennial Commission (ARBC) and later chairman of the American Revolution Bicentennial Board, made the case against a single site in a speech before Congress, December 10, 1970: "Every state would welcome international visitors. Every visitor would appreciate the rich diversity of our land. Every city needs urban renewal funds. Should we then in good faith allocate enormous sums of money for pavilions when so many urgent needs cry out for attention? I think not."

A Decision Is Made

On May 16, 1972, during its meeting in Boston, the ARBC rejected the proposal submitted by the Philadelphia 1976 Bicentennial Corporation for an international exposition in Philadelphia and so advised the President.

On July 4, 1972, President Nixon issued an unprecedented *Invitation to the World* to take part in the nationwide celebration. Noting that America is and always has been a nation of nations, the President said:

"Our Bicentennial Era is a time for America to say to the nations of the world 'You helped to make us what we are. Come and see what wonders your countrymen have worked in this new country of ours. Come and let us say thank you. Come and join in our celebration of a proud past. Come and share our dreams of a brighter future.' "

Ranged along the sidelines while the debate raged as how best to celebrate America's 200th anniversary, foreign nations and their people were understandably reluctant to make plans. They were hesitant to participate in a nationwide program, which was totally new in concept, until they were sure there wouldn't be a "centerpiece" in which they would be expected to make an investment.

As America's Bicentennial took shape and form, foreign governments moved forward with their plans, accepting and adopting the watchword "participation." Twenty-seven nations even formed official Bicentennial committees to help move things along.

A dramatic example of international cooperation and participation unfolded on July 4, 1976, when hundreds of sailing vessels, including most of the tall ships of the world, paraded in New York Harbor. Flying their national flags, the canvas-rigged ships glided past 49 warships of 25 nations which had assembled the day before in the largest ever peacetime International Naval Review. This scene, carried throughout the United States and overseas by television, epitomized the entwined histories of the world's peoples and the international character of the Bicentennial. Several hundred diplomatic representatives to the United States witnessed the panorama of sail from the deck of the aircraft carrier *U.S.S. Forrestal,* in company with President Gerald R. Ford and ARBA Administrator John W. Warner.

OPSAIL '76 and the International Naval Review: *(clockwise, beginning at top) Norway's* Christian Radich, *OPSAIL flag, Brazilian sailors, Captain von Stackelberg of the German bark,* Gorch Fock, *Japanese training ship,* Kapoii

Another dramatic example, this time abroad. The Federal Republic of Germany pulled out all the stops to help us commemorate. More than 4,000 Bicentennial-related events took place in that country in 1976 alone. They ranged from seminars for history teachers to presentations of American music and lectures on American Indians. They included concerts featuring American artists and musical groups, American art exhibitions, literary discussions and cooperation with American Army units stationed there. Activities such as these were commonplace in other countries as well.

(clockwise, beginning upper left) Deed to George Washington's ancestral home in England; crew of British OPSAIL ship, Sir Winston Churchill; Expo '74, Spokane, Washington; ARBA presentation ceremony to Around the World Auto Race; Don Quixote sculpture presented to the John F. Kennedy Center, Washington, D.C., by Spain

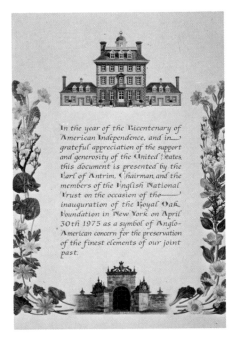

Taking Us Back to Our Roots

Many nations, noting how the Bicentennial was whetting the appetite of Americans for knowledge and understanding of their own particular ethnic, racial and regional heritages, decided to share their art and culture by sending exhibits and performing groups.

How to make such a contribution presented its own brand of problems. For many, particularly the smaller nations, the answer lay with the Smithsonian Institution's *Festival of American Folklife,* held annually on the Mall in the nation's capital.

With the ARBC and the ARBA providing over $1.3 million from their limited grant money between 1973 and 1976, the Smithsonian expanded the *Old Ways in the New World* portion of the festival to include performing groups from over 40 nations. At the ARBA's behest and with its funding, many of these visiting performers toured towns and cities across the nation. They reunited thousands of Americans with their cultural past and gave others a basis for understanding and enjoying the ethnic heritages of their neighbors. Sixty-one communities hosted groups on tour in 1976.

In some cities the Old Ways performances were made part of existing festivals, as in the case of the *Chicago International Trade Exposition.* Other cities created activities around their guests. St. George Orthodox Church served as the focal point for community activities when Lebanese folk performers traveled to El Paso, Texas.

During the expanded, three month long folklife festival in Washington, D.C. in 1976, the African Diaspora presented cultural heritages of Black Americans in a three-pronged representation.

Realistic settings vividly portrayed three aspects of their heritage: a rural Black church in the United States, a Caribbean marketplace and an African house. Cooks from three continents prepared such dishes as bitter leaf soup from Ghana, which has a taste much like that of our own south's collard greens.

(this page, opposite page) U.S. communities play host to America's cultural cousins

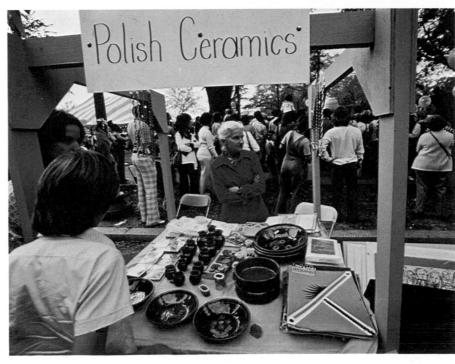

Foreigners Fête America

The Smithsonian Institution Traveling Exhibition Service (SITES), aided with funds from the ARBA, took on the task of routing exhibits from abroad throughout the country.

For the most part, rather than having all the countries trace their influence in American history, an effort was made to encourage foreign countries to loan artistic and historic treasures which might never be available except on a special occasion like the Bicentennial.

Many of the governments who were participating in this International Salute to the States did send national treasures of such importance that they had never been exhibited outside their countries.

A Cultural Medley

In one approach, exhibits were matched to American regions where a foreign country's influence was the greatest. For example, *The Dream of America: Swedish Emigration to the United States* was exhibited in the American Swedish Institute in Minneapolis, Minnesota. But in most instances, the aim was simply to acquaint Americans with as many of the cultures in their heritage as possible. This they did, as a medley of cultural exhibits toured the nation.

The International Salute to the States included exhibits such as *The Dutch Republic in the Days of John Adams, 1775–1795,* depicting the world of late 18th century Holland as John Adams knew it.

Argentina's exhibit, *Silverworks from Rio de la Plata, Argentina,* consisted of 175 ecclesiastical and secular silver objects typical of Argentine life during the 18th and 19th centuries. Household objects such as trays, candelabras and incense burners, and the daggers, silver spurs and bridle chains used by the gauchos, the Argentine cowboys, were included.

In *The Fourth Part of the World,* Australia related the exploration of Australia to similar developments in American history, featuring the migrations of early man as well as the coming of European explorers.

Among Belgium's exhibits were *Antwerp Drawings and Prints from the Sixteenth and Seventeenth Centuries* and *Belgian Gunmaking and American History.* Artists who were represented in the drawings and prints from Antwerp included Jacob Jordaens, Marten de Vos, Sir Anthony Van Dyck and Peter Paul Rubens. The gunmaking exhibit showed relations between American and Belgian arms manufacturers during the last 200 years.

Canada sent two touring exhibits. One, *Pitseolak: A Retrospective,* featured drawings by one of Canada's leading Eskimo graphic artists. The second showed Canadian history and topography as they were recorded in 100 watercolors, drawings and prints from the 18th and 19th centuries, part of *The W. H. Coverdale Collection of Canadiana.*

Treasures of Cyprus included objects from 6000 B.C. to the present.

An exhibit showing Shaker influence on Danish furniture was the theme of Denmark's *An American Inspiration: Danish Modern and Shaker Design.*

Finland's treasures—35 icons, most of them from the 18th century—were representative of the sacred figures and events of Eastern Orthodox Christianity.

Treasures of London was reported to be the "best collection of British silver ever to visit the U.S." It covered 500 years of British silver and included both antique and modern pieces.

Three hundred locks of all kinds, dating from the early Islamic period to the early 20th century, were included in *Locks from Iran: Pre-Islamic to 20th Century,* which were loaned by Iran for exhibit in the United States.

An exhibition from the Munch Museum in Oslo, Norway featured *Edvard Munch: The Major Graphics.*

Switzerland provided historical views of children's playthings in an exhibition called *Toys from Switzerland,* which was mounted in two versions.

Roman, Vandal and Byzantine mosaics revealed, in the *Tunisian Mosaics* exhibit, scenes of everyday life.

The first major exhibition of its kind from Yugoslavia to tour the United States, *Naïve Art in Yugoslavia* included 70 paintings and 20 wooden sculptures from the Gallery of Primitive Art in Zagreb, the first gallery in the world devoted to naïve art.

These are but a small sampling of the 30 major exhibitions managed by SITES and seen by Americans around the country during the Bicentennial, courtesy of foreign nations.

And There Was Still More . . .

Americans also played host to many of the world's most famous and prestigious performing arts groups during the Bicentennial.

Opera buffs were thrilled when Italy's La Scala Opera came—lock, stock and stage settings—for their first-ever performance in the United States. Other internationally renowned groups included the Vienna Philharmonic Orchestra; the Royal Danish Ballet;

Russia's Bolshoi Opera, Bolshoi Ballet and the Leningrad Symphony; the Paris Opera; the Berlin Philharmonic; the London Symphony and London Philharmonic; the Australian Ballet; the Abbey Players from Ireland; the Israeli Philharmonic; the State of Mexico Symphony Orchestra; the Polish Mime Ballet Theatre; the Romanian Zambir Gypsy Company; and the Netherlands National Ballet.

The Canadian Bicentennial Festival of Performing Arts, which took place at the Kennedy Center and the National Theater in Washington, D.C. in October 1975, was the largest ever mounted by the Canadians outside of Canada and the largest festival ever put on by one country at the center.

(clockwise, beginning upper left) Canadians present Eskimo sculpture for World Sculpture Garden in Philadelphia; U.S. and Canadian citizens join hands across Rainbow Bridge, Niagara Falls, New York; La Scala opera company from Milan, Italy performs Macbeth; visiting Royal Jordanian Band performs at 3rd Century America, Cape Canaveral, Florida

231

232 The Bicentennial Goes Abroad

International participation in the Bicentennial was a two-way street, and the ARBA's role as coordinator and catalyst went in two directions.

In terms of money, time and effort, the ARBA's greatest single contribution overseas was the creation and tour of *The World of Franklin and Jefferson* exhibit in 1975. It went to Paris, Warsaw and London before it opened in the United States in 1976.

The exhibition was designed by the office of Charles and Ray Eames for the ARBA, with the cooperation of the Metropolitan Museum of Art in New York, and with a grant from the International Business Machines Corporation (IBM). The exhibit, spanning 120 years of American history, set records for attendance in all three cities.

The ARBA's International Section helped work out the details and arrangements for other American exhibitions and cultural and musical performances in foreign nations.

One such exhibit, heralded on both sides of the Atlantic as the most important collection of North American Indian art ever assembled for international showing, opened at the Hayward Galleries in London in October 1976.

Organized by Ralph T. Coe, assistant director of the William Nelson Rockhill Gallery of Art and Mary Atkins Museum of Fine Art in Kansas City, Missouri, *Sacred Circles: 2000 Years of North American Indian Art* was jointly sponsored by the prestigious Arts Council of Great Britain and the British-American Associates. The ARBA assisted in arranging for its transport to England.

On April 15, 1975, the ARBA gave official recognition to a proposed *American Bicentennial National Park* in Israel, sponsored by the Jewish National Fund, which expected to raise the approximately $6 million needed through donations no larger than $3. The park, dedicated on July 4, 1976, links a large region southwest of Jerusalem with 200 years of American independence.

The ARBA also granted official recognition to Bicentennial projects of the Ninety-Nines, an international nonprofit association of licensed women pilots. In addition to cleaning up and beautifying airports, they planted an International Forest of Friendship in Atchison, Kansas in memory of aviatrix Amelia Earhart, who was born there.

The special interests of the world's philatelists were also considered by the ARBA. Special awards for Bicentennial collections at various stamp shows, plus an official engraved souvenir card produced by the Bureau of the Mint for *Interphil '76,* the only international stamp show held in 1976, were provided by the ARBA. The Bicentennial Philatelic Championship, awarded at Interphil, which was held in Philadelphia, May 28 to June 6, 1976, was won by Wallace F. Tolman of Camarillo, California for his exhibit: *U.S. Cancellations and Covers Portraying the Spirit of '76.*

ARBA Gives Due Recognition

Over 100 organizations, foreign and domestic, which sponsored activities abroad, were officially recognized for their Bicentennial efforts under a program established to encourage mutual understanding and cooperation through international activities pertinent to the Bicentennial commemoration.

The Australian-American Association, first overseas group recognized, held an *Australian-American Festival* in Sydney from March 27 through April 24, 1976. The festival included local performances of American plays, publication of a book on American history, exhibits of American Indian crafts, parades and even square-dancing.

Vice President Nelson A. Rockefeller and John Warner journeyed to Sydney to open the festivities. For Warner, it was the sixth foreign nation he had visited to take part in Bicentennial events. Others were Japan, Canada, England, France and Poland.

The Bicentennial was replete with international conferences tied to the historic milestone. They ranged from the *International World Congress on Philosophy of Law and Social Philosophy* in St. Louis during August of 1975 to a *World Food Conference* at Iowa State University in Ames, Iowa in late June and early July 1976. Most of the countries belonging to the United Nations participated in the conference.

Birthday Presents, Too

In keeping with the *Horizons '76* theme of the Bicentennial, there were lasting reminders from foreign nations for the appreciation and enjoyment of future generations of Americans. Some samples:
—Japanese citizens donated a priceless collection of bonsai trees to the National

Arboretum in Washington, D.C., as well as a new 500 seat experimental theater on the top floor of the Kennedy Center. The Japanese also contributed a total of 2,000 cherry trees for planting in San Francisco, Los Angeles and Seattle.
—Private citizens from the Netherlands donated a million tulip bulbs for planting in 100 American communities.
—From the Federal Republic of Germany came a sophisticated planetarium-projector system for the Einstein Spacearium in the Smithsonian's new National Air and Space Museum in Washington, D.C.
—Great Britain contributed the Bicentennial Bell, which was unveiled by Queen Elizabeth II on July 6, 1976. The bell, now hanging in the orientation center at Independence National Historical Park in Philadelphia, is similar to the Liberty Bell and was cast in the same foundry in London as the original.
—Some governments chose to enhance mutual understanding through educational programs. Australia established a Chair in Australian Studies at Harvard University; Canada provided a $50,000 grant to the Center of Canadian Studies at Johns Hopkins School of Advanced International Studies; the Federal Republic of Germany endowed a permanent Theodor Heuss Chair at the Graduate School of Political and Social Science at the New School for Social Research in New York City and a Konrad Adenauer Chair for a visiting professor at Georgetown University in Washington, D.C.; Iran established a Bicentennial Scholarship Program to assist Americans studying in Iran.

Tourists All

The people-to-people aspects of the Bicentennial provided much of the international flavor. Sister Cities International, a program which matches a foreign city with an American counterpart, reported a dramatic upswing in the exchange of people and activities among cities here and abroad. SCI was officially recognized by the ARBA for its Bicentennial hospitality efforts. Its president, Louis Wozar of Dayton, Ohio, said:

"At no time in its twenty-year history has the U.S. Sister City program experienced such a mass influx of visitors from its counterpart affiliates throughout the world."

A typical example: New Holland, Pennsylvania had a genuine French flavor to its Bicentennial weekend festivities when 120 citizens from its Sister City, Longvic, France, came to help the townsfolk celebrate. Similar scenes occurred hundreds of times during the Bicentennial.

The United States Travel Service reported foreign tourism up 12 percent during the first nine months of 1976, on top of an 11.2 percent increase in 1975. All told, almost 30 million visitors came to the country during the 21 month period of heaviest Bicentennial activity.

Because of keen interest in visiting the U.S., the ARBA was actively involved in all aspects of tourism during the Bicentennial. Special efforts were made to help and encourage host cities to improve facilities and services for foreign visitors.

To help foreigners decide where they wanted to go, the ARBA joined in sponsoring the travels of 400 foreign journalists from 50 nations, and their families, across the United States. The eight, one month Bicentennial tours enabled them to report on the American celebration to their readers back home.

(opposite page, clockwise, beginning upper left) Sister Cities join Bicentennial: New Holland, Pennsylvania and Longvic, France; Seattle, Washington (ceremony, with King Olav V of Norway on the right) and Beyen Place, Norway; Salt Lake City, Utah and Matsumoto, Japan; Alexandria, Virginia and Dundee, Scotland; New Holland, Pennsylvania and Longvic, France. (this page, clockwise, beginning upper right) Rochester, New York salutes its Sister Cities; Austrians visit Washington, D.C.; Roanoke, Virginia and Wonju, Korea; Sister Cities Bridge in Rochester, New York; Tirolean dancers

Praise from Foreign Press

The reaction by foreign media to America's Bicentennial weekend celebration provides another means of measuring the importance and impact of the Bicentennial abroad.

Around the world, the celebration of the 200th anniversary of the United States was greeted in large measure with affection and enthusiasm. There were acknowledgments of the sacrifices of its people and their contributions to world security and well-being. There were expressions of hope that the nation would continue to play a dominant role in world affairs and affirmations of the validity of a political system that has survived 200 years of growth and travail.

Noting the mood of America, a West German TV commentator, reporting from Washington, D.C., told his listeners: "July 4, 1976, was one of the most peaceful holidays in U.S. history . . . July 5 was a day of contented remembrance. They all enjoyed the feeling of standing in the center of the world. . . ."

Carl Weiss, another West German TV commentator, observed: "Historians and critics have again and again emphasized that—after Vietnam and Watergate—the Bicentennial has no theme, perspective, ideal and sense, but the July 4 weekend is about to remove all doubts: Joy and optimism and an intractable pride are dominating."

The (London) Observer said: "The Fourth of July cannot be our feast. . . . But we can be a little proud that no other nation, not even imperial Rome, produced so great and nobly independent an offspring."

In Italy, the *Corriere della Sera* of Milan wrote: "Behind the picturesque and commercial façade of ceremonies and commemorations, the Bicentennial is a confirmation of the validity of a political system which for two centuries has withstood severest trials and absorbed the deepest social and economic transformations."

In Tokyo, the newspaper *Yomiuri Shimbun* commented: ". . . the great confusion in which U.S. society was thrown for some time, appears to have nearly ended, thus proving once again that the country is capable of healing its wounds."

In Korea, the semiofficial *Kyunghyang Shinmun* said: "Our concern focuses on the future of America rather than its past. . . ."

In Iran, the magazine *Khandaniha* wrote: "The world without the United States would be devoid of right, law, moral restraints, security and liberty . . . The United States and its people are necessary for the security, liberty, independence and economic well-being of most countries, just as air and water are essential to life. . . ."

In Belgium, *La Dernière Heure* of Brussels said: "America remains the safest ally—it has proved it—of our free Western nations."

Also in Brussels, *Le Peuple,* under a title that read "Thank you, Sammy," declared: "In these days of fervent celebration we want to think with emotion of the tens of thousands of boys who sleep under the marble which covers each American tomb in the U.S. cemeteries of Europe rather than of Watergate or neocapitalism."

El Mercurio of Chile commented: "The whole world is part of this commemoration and this is logical because never before in history has a nation reached such a universal presence. . . ."

In Ecuador, Quito's leading daily, *El Mercurio,* said: ". . . It is just to recognize the greatness created exactly 200 years ago in the important and inspirational Declaration of Independence. . . ."

In Mexico, the newspaper *Excelsior* said: "Two centuries later the U.S. is the center of universal power, faithful to its principles expressed in its Constitution. . . ." The newspaper *Novedades* observed: "In spite of so many errors committed by the U.S., the American celebration of the Bicentennial adds to their durability and grandness. . . ."

The newspaper *Musawat* in Pakistan hailed the United States as "the greatest upholder of freedom and equality in the free world," adding, "The contribution made by the American people for the promotion of democratic traditions will remain enshrined in golden letters in world history. . . ."

The Swedish *Dagens Nyheter* said: "It is the variety of American society that even the strongest critic of the U.S. must take into account. Everyone can find some corner in which to do his own thing. . . ."

In New Delhi, *The Times of India* titled its editorial: "The American Bicentennial: Recovery from Doubts and Despair," and observed: ". . . no other country is as vigorous, innovative, productive and well placed to influence the course of events in the coming years and decades."

In Brazil, the newspaper *O Estado de São Paulo* wrote: "In the past two centuries . . . thanks to the democratic ideal of 1776 . . . the U.S. has been able to overcome the greatest domestic crises and engage in the international power game without any digression from democratic principles. . . ."

In Argentina, the influential *La Prensa* commented that the U.S. Bicentennial should inspire other American republics to "return to the mainspring of our freedom. . . ."

The Danish newspaper *Aktuelt* wrote: "In the course of time we have bawled out the U.S.A. . . . Today, it is a pleasure to say 'Happy Birthday America' because all of us are under great obligations to the Americans. . . ."

An Austrian daily, *Arbeiter-Zeitung,* editorialized: "Despite all errors, weaknesses and crises, the vitality of the United States is unsapped. The Free World, which ought to be very grateful to America, and not only for Marshall Plan aid, will need the United States also in the future as well."

In the Soviet Union, official organs like *Pravda, Izvestia* and *Literaturnaya Gazeta* carried generally favorable references to the Bicentennial.

In Zaire in Africa, the Kinshasa *Elima,* while pointing to some shortcomings in American foreign policy, noted: "Moreover, as residents of the third world, we must particularly praise the positive response made by America to the appeal of the underdeveloped world. . . ."

And so the world was listening when President Ford spoke at Independence Hall in Philadelphia on Bicentennial Day, July 4, 1976:

"The world knows where we stand. The world is ever conscious of what Americans are doing for better or for worse because the United States today remains the most successful realization of humanity's universal hope.

"The world may or may not follow, but we lead because our whole history says we must. Liberty is for all men and women as a matter of equal and unalienable right. The establishment of justice and peace abroad will in large measure depend upon the peace and justice we create here in our own country, where we still show the way."

"American Show Ends in Moscow"   237

The American wire service, Associated Press, filed this story on December 13, 1976:

"MOSCOW, Dec. 13 (AP)—Russians yelled and pleaded with police not to be turned away as the American Bicentennial exhibition closed its doors tonight after a one-month run that was a sensation in Moscow.

"The U.S. Information Agency exhibit in Moscow's Sokolniki Park attracted 270,000 visitors despite freezing weather, five-hour lines and two bomb scares. People were still waiting to get in at the final closing time."

Peace Arch, Blaine, Washington

The Federal
Bicentennial
Agencies

240   When ARBA Administrator John W. Warner submitted the first American Revolution Bicentennial Administration (ARBA) report to Congress in August 1975, he predicted a Bicentennial commemoration which "befits the greatness and the dignity of our nation."

The forecast was based upon a deep personal awareness of a national Bicentennial spirit that had been developing since 1966 when the American Revolution Bicentennial Commission (ARBC) came into being.

Early Planning

Early planning for the celebration of the Bicentennial of the United States of America had begun amidst a background of national divisiveness and uncertainty. Few agreed—including those involved in its planning—what form the Bicentennial commemoration should take. Yet there was a strong current of public commitment to some kind of celebration. Despite early apathy and public disinterest, there was a constancy to Bicentennial planning that eventually led to one of the most impressive expressions of national pride in the country's history.

The American Revolution Bicentennial Commission (ARBC) (1966–1974)

Much public debate had occurred during the 1960's over whether or not there should be a giant single-event celebration of the nation's 200th birthday. For at least a decade, the city of Philadelphia had been developing and redeveloping several plans for hosting an international exposition in 1976. This matter had not been resolved by the time President Lyndon B. Johnson signed Public Law 89–491, which established the ARBC on July 4, 1966.

The legislation had been submitted by the Johnson administration and was substantially similar to bills earlier introduced by two U.S. Representatives, Charles McC. Mathias (R-Md) and F. Bradford Morse (R-Mass).

The ARBC was born during a period which saw a nation divided over the war in Vietnam, dissatisfaction with many of our institutions and uneasiness among a majority of the people—particularly among youth.

The ARBC's Two Phases

The ARBC, whose mandate was amended by Congress several times, had two distinct functional phases— planning and implementation. Two successive chairmen led the ARBC during the planning phase and one during implementation.

The ARBC, as organized during the Johnson Administration, began the first step of the planning phase under the chairmanship of Carlisle H. Humelsine, 52, a leader in the field of historic preservation and president of Colonial Williamsburg in Virginia.

Planning continued under the ARBC with changes in membership made by the new President, Richard M. Nixon. He appointed a new chairman—Dr. J. E. Wallace Sterling, 62, a Canadian-born American and chancellor of Stanford University in California.

The Sterling-led ARBC concentrated on the preparation and submission of the Report to the President, as required by law, which would become the basic plan for the commemoration.

After submission of the Bicentennial planning report, Dr. Sterling resigned. On September 11, 1970, David J. Mahoney, 47, New York-based chairman of the board and chief executive officer of Norton Simon, Inc., a widely-known conglomerate, was appointed chairman. The ARBC then entered its second phase, that of implementation of plans and coordination of Bicentennial activities.

(opposite page, left) Launching the Bicentennial Era, July 1971, at the National Archives; (right top) David J. Mahoney receiving gift of bells from Mrs. Robyna Ketchum of Cos Cob, Connecticut; (right bottom) Mahoney with former President Nixon after Air Force One was renamed "Spirit of '76"

The Humelsine Years (1967-1969)

As organized in 1966, the ARBC had 34 members. Seventeen were government officials and 17 represented the public. The 17 government members consisted of four senators and four representatives and nine ex officio members providing support from various parts of the federal government: the Secretary of State, the Attorney General, the Secretary of the Interior, the Secretary of Defense, the Secretary of Health, Education and Welfare, the Librarian of Congress, the Secretary of the Smithsonian Institution, the Archivist of the United States and the Chairman of the Federal Council on the Arts and the Humanities.

One of the 17 public members, Carlisle Humelsine, was designated chairman by President Johnson on January 23, 1967. The oath of office to the public members was administered by Vice President Hubert H. Humphrey.

Of the original ARBC members, six were Virginians, two were associated with leading universities (Brandeis and Tuskegee Institute) and two were former presidents of the American Bar Association. Others included the director of the Houston Museum of Fine Arts; a retired Air Force general; the president of Steuben Glass Company; the editor/publisher of a newspaper in Nebraska, who was also a former Secretary of the Interior; the president

and chairman of the board of Litton Industries; and three authors.

At the first full ARBC meeting on February 22, 1967, the group urged Congress to amend the legislation to authorize appropriations to provide for a full-time staff to support the planning efforts of the part-time, unpaid public members.

But the government, beset by other, larger problems, gave low priority to the financial and staff needs of an organization that was planning the commemoration of the nation's birthday, nine years away.

First Funding

Seventeen months were to pass before Congress acted on the ARBC's request for funds for staff support. On July 9, 1968, $150,000 was appropriated for staff and operating funds (Public Law 90–392).

Shortly thereafter, on October 9, 1968, the ARBC had its second meeting and hired the first executive director, Richard W. Barrett. However, the ARBC postponed hiring a permanent staff until its interim report could be submitted to the President.

One of the first actions of the ARBC was to approve motions supporting the U.S. Olympics Committee's proposal to have Los Angeles and Denver designated as the 1976 sites for the Summer and Winter Olympics respectively.

The members also voted at the October meeting to submit their resignations to whoever would be the next President. Richard M. Nixon was elected to the Presidency in 1968, took office in January 1969 but did not act on the ARBC for six months. This inaction effectively left it in limbo, causing Bicentennial planning to come to a halt for nine months.

The Sterling Year (1969–1970)

The President announced the public membership of a reorganized ARBC on July 3, 1969. Seven of the original commissioners were reappointed, and Dr. Wallace Sterling was named as the chairman. This dedicated Californian had an immediate and pressing priority—to produce the nation's Bicentennial plan as required by law. Chairman Sterling appointed Melbourne L. Spector as the new executive director.

In his announcement, President Nixon set a new tone for the celebration: "it [the celebration] belongs not only to the 13 original states, but equally to the newest and the farthest from those 18th century battlefields. It is a national celebration, a national anniversary; it challenges each of the 50 states, and every community, to look to its heritage and its hopes."

The President's approach was not immediately followed, as the ARBC, under Dr. Sterling's leadership, still faced the issue of whether or not to recommend a single site international exposition. Opponents and supporters drew battle lines, and the cities of Miami, Boston, Philadelphia and Washington, D.C. competed for designation as the site for hosting an expo.

While attempting to resolve issues such as the exposition question, the design of an official Bicentennial symbol and relations with the media, the ARBC labored long and hard at producing the required report. It was no easy task and took months of hard work. The slow progress was due in part to those earlier delays in appointing the first commissioners and in providing funds for a staff.

The ARBC under Dr. Sterling set the stage for many of the programs and activities which became the basis for the final plans for the celebration. The time span for celebrating the Bicentennial was recommended as 1970 to 1987. The ARBC proposed a cooperative relationship with local, state and private Bicentennial commissions, under which the ARBC would provide assistance and guidance to the extent possible.

The ARBC submitted its Bicentennial planning report to the President on July 4, 1970. Having accomplished his original objective, Dr. Sterling resigned as chairman.

The report and the President's affirmative transmittal message to the Congress outlined the Bicentennial goal: to forge a new national commitment—a new "Spirit of '76"—that would unite the nation in purpose and dedication to the advancement of human welfare as the United States moved into its third century.

(below) ARBC headquarters, 736 Jackson Place, N.W., Washington, D.C.

(opposite page) The national Bicentennial symbol, animated for use on television

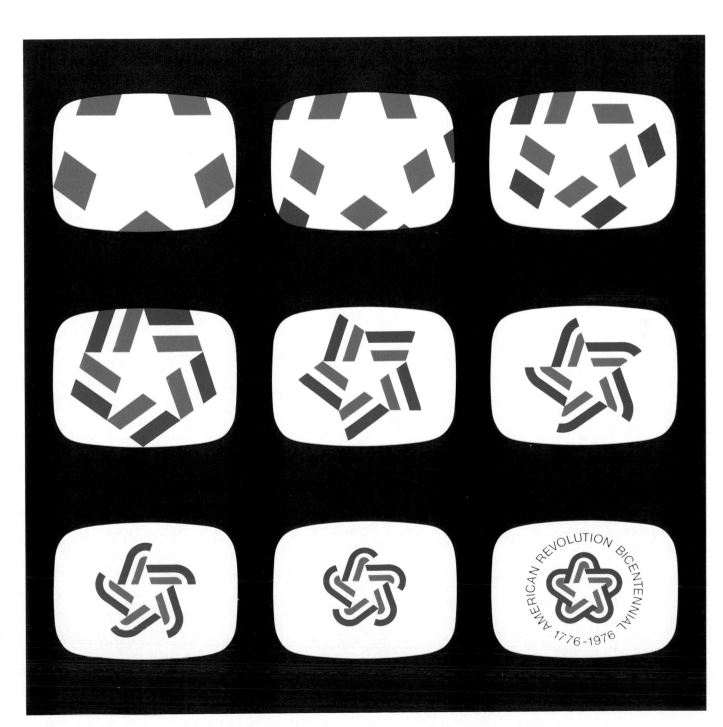

Three Celebration Themes

To advance this concept, the ARBC proposed three themes to guide the celebration:

Heritage '76, encouraging Americans and the world to examine the nation's past and develop historical perspectives from which to appraise its origins, values and accomplishments.

Open House USA (later changed to *Festival USA*), a sharing of America and its geographic attractions and cultural diversity with the American people and their friends around the world.

Horizons '76, a look to the future— Americans were asked to accomplish, by 1976, at least one major project that would be a lasting contribution to the American way of life.

Expo Registration

The President's message to Congress explained that he had instructed the Secretary of State to proceed with appropriate registration procedures with the Bureau of International Expositions in Paris, France for an exposition to be held in Philadelphia. The President added, "Such an exposition, however, is to be primarily cultural, inspirational and noncommercial in character, with the emphasis on quality rather than size."

The Mahoney Years (1970–1973)

On September 11, 1970, the same day President Nixon transmitted the ARBC's report to Congress, the President began to take steps toward implementation of the recommendations. He appointed David J. Mahoney ARBC chairman.

Bringing a successful background in corporate management to the ARBC's day-to-day operations, Chairman Mahoney worked to put into effect the national plan for the Bicentennial.

Chairman Mahoney broadened the dialogue with the American people by holding ARBC meetings in San Francisco, Dallas, Chicago and Boston during 1971 and 1972. The ARBC heard firsthand from state organizers, local community leaders and individuals about their vision of what the Bicentennial should or should not be. Special interest groups, citizen organizations, youth and ethnic-racial groups were also heard.

Enlarging the ARBC

In response to strong feelings expressed to it by a number of youth representatives, the ARBC submitted proposals for enlarging the commission with eight additional public members. Congress authorized the additional membership in Public Law 92–236. A varied group of appointees was subsequently named.

In October 1971, Chairman Mahoney announced the opening of ARBC regional offices in Atlanta, Boston, Chicago and San Francisco to assist states and local communities in their planning. In November, Chairman Mahoney named Jack I. LeVANT as executive director of the staff.

Bicentennial Parks

During January and February of 1972, the ARBC developed an alternative to the international exposition concept. Called Bicentennial Parks, the plan called for the development of a cultural-recreational park in each of the 50 states. The park would serve as the focus of a state's participation in the Bicentennial and as a lasting remembrance of the celebration afterward.

At a joint meeting of the ARBC and the state commissions on February 21, 1972, Chairman Mahoney dramatically unveiled a model of a prototypical Bicentennial park. The ARBC voted to proceed with a full-scale feasibility study. The National Governors'

(opposite page, left) ARBC communications kits, issued in 1973; (right) ARBC exhibit

(below) Model of a Bicentennial park

246 Conference, which was meeting in an adjoining ballroom of the hotel at the same time, adopted a resolution supporting the park concept.

National or Local Celebration?

Time passed, and a grassroots Bicentennial observance began to emerge. The ARBC had informally agreed in 1971 to continue studying the idea of a major, single-focus celebration in Philadelphia. But time was running out, and a decision had to be made. What would a giant exposition cost? Would it have the active support of local citizens? Was there enough time left to stage it and to involve foreign nations?

Philadelphia, the city that hosted the 1876 exposition, had been planning such an event officially and unofficially since 1956. Proposed sites included the Delaware River front, space created over railroad tracks, a 1,000 acre mental hospital farm and the city landfill area. Final cost for the exposition had been estimated at $1.5 to $2.1 billion.

As the commissioners pondered these questions at their May 15–16, 1972 meeting in Boston, all the evidence seemed to point to a negative. With some misgivings, the ARBC voted unanimously against an international exposition in Philadelphia in 1976.

The director of the U.S. Office of Management and Budget advised the President to concur with the ARBC's actions. On May 22, President Nixon told Congress, "Under the full weight of these recommendations, I have reluctantly concluded that we cannot prudently go forward with the international exposition in Philadelphia."

At the Boston meeting, the ARBC also unanimously approved a *National Historic Records Program,* which had as its goal locating and preserving state and local historical records. Congress later implemented this proposal by expanding the functions of the existing National Historical Publications Commission and redesignating it as the National Historical Publications and Records Commission.

The Public Debate

Spring and summer of 1972 brought a surge of public interest and comment on official Bicentennial management and planning. The ARBC was considering proposals for many different programs and found itself confronted by many different critics, each with a particular point of view. Some objected to the Philadelphia expo, others to the Bicentennial parks proposal, still others to the grassroots approach.

Closed sessions at the ARBC's meetings led to demands for the release of meeting transcripts. The ARBC's dialogues on these troublesome issues, as recorded in the somewhat confusing transcripts, did not clarify matters when they were subsequently released.

Several national magazines and newspapers featured articles about the various program proposals and the ARBC's apparent inability to make final decisions on them. The tide crested around July 4, 1972, a time when reader interest was naturally focused on Bicentennial planning.

The Senate Judiciary Committee's Subcommittee on Federal Charters, Holidays and Celebrations reacted to the stories by calling for full-scale public hearings on the ARBC, its proposals and its staff leadership. ARBC Executive Director Jack LeVANT, a target of some of the criticism, resigned July 31, 1972, the day before the hearings began, helping to defuse the crisis.

There was more to come. In mid-August a series of three stories in issues of *The Washington Post* aimed charges at the ARBC, based on documents which came from ARBC files. The articles made charges of "politics, commercialism and jingoism."

The documents had come into the hands of Jeremy Rifkin, leader of a self-proclaimed "New Left" movement, the People's Bicentennial Commission. While containing no substantiation of wrongdoing, the papers and letters were damaging when quoted out of context.

The *Post* articles were published on the very days the House of Representatives was preparing to vote on funds to operate the ARBC. In view of the allegations, the House appropriated funds for ARBC operations only until February 1973.

In the meantime, the House Judiciary Committee staff was ordered to undertake a full investigation of the problems detailed in the *Post* series.

At about the same time, Senator Mathias, later an ARBC commissioner, asked the General Accounting Office to investigate the ARBC's operations.

The Department of the Interior, which was responsible for the ARBC's housekeeping operations, independently began its own informal investigation into the allegations.

Working under these handicaps, the ARBC nevertheless continued to plan the Bicentennial.

One of the most important ARBC decisions was made at the November 15, 1972 meeting. At that time, the ARBC decided that its role would be essentially passive—coordinating and encouraging Bicentennial activities, rather than playing an active operational role. A motion was approved which stated, "It shall be the policy of the ARBC to assume operational responsibility for a particular program only when specifically authorized by Congress." This motion would provide the basic policy direction for both the ARBC and later for the ARBA.

Clearing the Air

The final reports of the congressional committees and other agencies which were conducting investigations of the ARBC all concluded that the basic charges of "politics, jingoism and commercialism" made against the ARBC were without foundation. These reports confirmed what the ARBC had long known: the unwieldy commission structure fragmented authority and responsibility, preventing effective and timely decisionmaking. Indeed, the ARBC itself had recommended in its 1970 Report to the President that it be dissolved and replaced by a new federal agency established by the Congress to complete the planning and execution of the celebration.

On February 1, 1973, President Nixon sent a message to Congress requesting the passage of legislation "to establish the American Revolution Bicentennial Administration (ARBA)." Chairman Mahoney and Vice-Chairman Hobart Lewis joined with the President in urging speedy congressional approval.

While awaiting congressional action on a new organizational structure, the ARBC revamped its chain of command, delegating authority to Acting Executive Director Hugh A. Hall, who had been named to succeed Jack LeVANT.

With the strong backing of Chairman Mahoney, the ARBC staff was able to speed up planning activities.

For instance: *Operation Sail-OPSAIL '76* was officially recognized; *Expo '74,* to be held in Spokane, Washington, was also officially recognized; and the formal authorization of what was to become the most successful vehicle for generating participation of the entire celebration, the *Bicentennial Communities Program,* was agreed to on March 26, 1973.

In this climate of positive actions, the Congress appropriated additional funds for the continued operation of the ARBC.

Resolving the Commercialism Issue

Allegations had been made of commercial exploitation of the Bicentennial. However, the General Accounting Office concluded from its review of the ARBC that "in planning, encouraging, developing, and coordinating activities commemorating the Bicentennial, the Commission and its staff have a responsibility to work with the business community as well as the general public. The fact that business firms may profit commercially from the Bicentennial does not relieve the Commission of its responsibility."

In particular, sales of memorabilia and souvenirs—both by state and local Bicentennial commissions and by the ARBC itself—would prove to be an important source of Bicentennial funding for state and local community projects.

The congressionally-authorized Commemorative Medals program, initiated by the ARBC in 1972, began to provide a source of revenues to support national, state and local activities.

The program began with the ARBC's first Philatelic-Numismatic Combination (PNC). As the first Bicentennial stamp and medal commemorative to be put on the market, this popular item was successful, producing a net return of $2.7 million.

Federal Programs Launched

These nonappropriated funds made it possible for the ARBC to stimulate Bicentennial activities in other agencies of the federal government.

ARBC commitment to the programs of other federal agencies came in the form of $1 million divided equally among the National Endowment for the Arts, the National Endowment for the Humanities, the National Science Foundation, the Smithsonian Institution and the National Historical Publications Commission.

Thus encouraged, these and other federal agencies began or continued their ambitious plans for a range of Bicentennial activities, with the ARBC playing a role in overall coordination.

ARBC Recap

The life of the ARBC was fast coming to an end. It could look back with pride at a number of significant accomplishments. Among others: a complete network of state Bicentennial commissions was in being; plans were underway for the involvement of ethnic-racial groups and young people; prototypes for major Bicentennial exhibits had been designed; a national recognition program was being initiated. In operation were a computer-automated master calendar and project registration system; a revenue-producing commemorative medals program; the *Bicentennial Communities Program;* and a network of 10 regional offices, one in each federal region, which were to serve state and local Bicentennial commissions.

But above all, a truly nationwide, grassroots commemoration of the nation's first 200 years had finally been launched.

On December 11, 1973, the President approved Public Law 93–179, abolishing the ARBC and establishing the ARBA, to become effective on January 11, 1974.

The American Revolution Bicentennial Administration (ARBA) (1974–1977)

The ARBA came into existence in 1974, shadowed by the gathering clouds of the Watergate scandal.

Hugh A. Hall was appointed by President Nixon as acting administrator, to serve until a permanent administrator was appointed.

The ARBA was the product of a consensus of the ARBC and the congressional and executive branches with respect to the proper role of the federal government in the Bicentennial. The experience of the years since the establishment of the ARBC in 1966 had clearly solidified agreement that no single governmental entity—federal or state—and no single geographic locality should dominate the Bicentennial.

Under Public Law 93–179, the basic role of the new agency was to stimulate, encourage and coordinate events, activities and projects of local, state, national and international significance sponsored by governmental and nongovernmental agencies.

In calling for a balanced Bicentennial commemoration encompassing the *Heritage '76, Festival USA* and *Horizons '76* themes, the law directed the ARBA as a primary function to ". . . prepare the master calendar of events of local, State, National, and international significance which will take place between March 1975 and December 31, 1976 . . . [and to] provide for the bicentennial master calendar or register of programs and projects, and in other ways provide a central clearinghouse for information and coordination. . . ."

The legislation also carried over to the ARBA the authority and responsibility of the ARBC with respect to official recognition of programs, public information and awareness efforts, the medals program and the matching grants program for state and local Bicentennial committees which was derived from nonappropriated revenues. In addition, it gave the ARBA the authority to license the use of the symbol by commercial organizations.

Pursuant to the law, the new ARBA firmly established these objectives: (1) that the federal government and the states should cooperate in a common effort and that each individual should have a right to participate; and (2) that federal funding in direct support of citizen programs initiated by local communities and groups should be divided as evenly as possible on a matching basis through Bicentennial organizations chartered in each of the states.

(below) ARBA's Bicentennial Communities exhibit

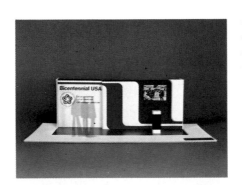

(clockwise, beginning upper left) ARBA airport exhibit; Bicentennial Information Network (BINET) publications; BINET demonstration; July 4, 1976 Bicentennial Weekend Information Center; The World of Franklin and Jefferson *exhibit; "Arba the Eagle" television personality; BINET quarterly publication*

250 **The American Revolution Bicentennial Board and Advisory Council**

The law created a Board to provide policy and guidelines for ARBA operations, to give final approval to all ARBA grants and to review and approve proposed ARBA annual budgets. The Board was to be bipartisan and to have 11 members: the ARBA administrator, two members from the U.S. House of Representatives, two U.S. Senators, the chairman and vice-chairman of the new Advisory Council, the Secretary of the Interior and three state Bicentennial commission officers.

Besides the administrator, other appointees were: Senator Edward W. Brooke (R-Mass), (subsequently elected chairman); Dr. J. Duane Squires of the New Hampshire American Revolution Bicentennial Commission, (subsequently elected vice-chairman); Senator Joseph M. Montoya (D-NM); Representative M.

Caldwell Butler (R-Va); Representative Lindy (Mrs. Hale) Boggs (D-La); Secretary of the Interior Rogers C. B. Morton (and later his successors, Stanley K. Hathaway, Thomas S. Kleppe, and Cecil D. Andrus); Carol L. Evans of the Michigan American Revolution Bicentennial Commission; Andrew McNally, III of the Illinois Bicentennial Commission; and the Chairman and Vice-Chairman of the ARB Advisory Council, David L. Wolper of California and Ann Hawkes Hutton of Pennsylvania, respectively. Mrs. Hutton had also served on the ARBC.

A 25 member Presidentially-appointed Advisory Council was established to advise the administrator. Council members, appointed from private life, provided the broad representation needed to reflect the diversity of the nation's Bicentennial planning. One member was a homemaker, two were students, four were writers, five were women, seven were executives.

Professionally, two were from the religious community, three represented the mass media and five were in education.

In addition to the chairman and vice-chairman named earlier, members included Maya Angelou; Anne L. Armstrong; William J. Baroody, Sr.; Laura Bergt; the Most Reverend Joseph L. Bernardin; Anna Chennault; Joan Ganz Cooney; Martin Diamond; Dr. Richard Gambino; David L. Hale; Alex P. Haley; Martin S. Hayden; Mrs. Lyndon B. Johnson; Hobart Lewis; Dr. F. David Mathews; James A. Michener; Lyle M. Nelson; L. Tom Perry; Dr. Jacinto J. Quirarte; Betty Shabazz; Frank Stanton; Jana E. Sutton; and Harry Van Arsdale, Jr.

Subsequent to their appointment, Anne Armstrong left the Council to become Ambassador to the Court of St. James and David Mathews to become Secretary of Health, Education and Welfare. C. Robertson Trowbridge joined the Council thereafter.

. . . and a New Leader

The Secretary of the Navy, John W. Warner, a lawyer and graduate of Washington and Lee University and the University of Virginia Law School, was nominated to become the first administrator. He was sworn in as head of the new agency on the steps of the United States Capitol on April 11, 1974 by Vice President Gerald R. Ford. Warner vowed to produce a nation of Bicentennial participants rather than one of spectators.

Building on the groundwork already laid by its predecessor and using the experience of the ARBC staff, the ARBA began to expand the concept of a celebration in which every American and every friend of the United States could participate.

Past, Present and Future

One of the new agency's objectives was to refine further the national Bicentennial themes already developed by the ARBC and to disseminate them.

Heritage '76 was defined as "Let Us Remember"—a nationwide summons to recall our heritage, to place it in its historical perspective and to focus on the origins, values and unfolding panorama of our nation's history.

Festival USA was defined as "Let Us Celebrate"—a nationwide opportunity to share with each other and the people of the world our traditions, our culture, our hospitality and our character.

Horizons '76 was defined as "Let Us Shape a Better Tomorrow"—a nationwide challenge to every American, acting as an individual or within the community, to select and act upon goals to make America become a more perfect union and to improve the quality of life for all as the nation enters its third century.

251

ARB Advisory Council members: (counter clockwise, beginning upper left) Martin Diamond; Harry Van Arsdale, Jr. and Alex P. Haley; Frank Stanton; The Most Reverend Joseph L. Bernardan and Dr. Richard Gambino. Vice President Ford at John W. Warner's swearing-in

(opposite page) The ARB Board

252   Clear Lines of Authority

The ARBA and the Board quickly got down to business with a clear-cut delineation of responsibility: the Board determining basic policy and the administrator having full authority for execution of that policy.

The ARBA adhered strictly to a policy of nonpartisanship in the affairs of the Bicentennial and also made a commitment to the principle that the blueprints for the celebration would be the three documents: the Declaration of Independence, the Constitution and the Bill of Rights.

The new agency also responded to critics who were denouncing the Bicentennial for lacking a "centerpiece" or "national focus." It did so by taking the position that the Bicentennial would involve *all* our communities, institutions and citizens. This was notwithstanding the fact that there was no precedent for a celebration that would take place in every corner of the nation.

Involving the People

Basic to this development was the *Bicentennial Communities Program,* first adopted by the ARBC and expanded by the ARBA to inspire the greatest number of citizens to participate. Over 90 percent of the nation's population was affected by or included in this extraordinarily successful program.

Following the ARB Board's philosophy of emphasizing the nation's cultural diversity, the ARBA convened a meeting in Washington on June 27, 1974 which led to the creation of the Bicentennial

Ethnic/Racial Coalition (BERC) shortly thereafter. On July 1, 1974, the ARBA also established a Native American Programs Office in Denver, Colorado to ensure that the often-neglected contributions of Native Americans to the development of American society would be recognized in the Bicentennial.

The popular character of the celebration was further reinforced the following year with the formation of five alliances, each bringing together organizations with similar interests for the purpose of promoting more widespread participation in the Bicentennial. The five encompassed service, hospitality, ethnic and racial, sports and business organizations, respectively.

(lower left) Vice President Rockefeller swears in Marjorie W. Lynch as deputy administrator; various ARBA management charts

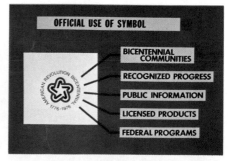

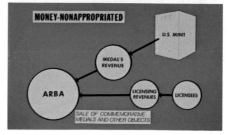

Federal Agency Programs

During its first year, the ARBA recognized the federal agencies who were eventually responsible for more than 200 Bicentennial programs proposed by federal agencies and departments. These programs varied, ranging from research by the Library of Congress into the origins and consequences of the American Revolution to the Department of Housing and Urban Development's program, *Horizons on Display,* developed in cooperation with the ARBA. The program highlighted 200 examples of how communities were successfully tackling their problems using their own resources and ingenuity.

Business Provides Money

The ARBA worked hard to encourage the commitment of private financial resources to Bicentennial projects. In time, 241 American business organizations committed $38.9 million. Many millions more were spent for which the ARBA has no record, as many businesses participated independently of the ARBA.

Federal and state appropriations during the earlier years of Bicentennial planning provided the seed money to establish official Bicentennial efforts in each of the states. However, most of the cost of Bicentennial projects and events was paid for by the private sector.

Freedom Train

The *American Freedom Train,* for example, was sponsored by the American Freedom Train Foundation with initial contributions, totaling $5 million, from the Prudential Insurance Company, Pepsico, General Motors and Kraftco.

The *Bicentennial Wagon Train Pilgrimage to Pennsylvania* was first funded by the Commonwealth of Pennsylvania, with an additional $2 million in money and services from the Gulf Oil Corporation and Encyclopaedia Britannica, Inc.

The Smithsonian Institution's *Festival of American Folklife* was a joint federal government-private sector venture. Contributions to the Smithsonian Institution included $1.325 million in nonappropriated funds from the ARBA and $1 million each from American Airlines, Inc. and General Foods Corporation.

The American Express Company paid for reglazing and refurbishing the Statue of Liberty, while the Crouse-Hinds Company of Syracuse, New York provided the New York Harbor lady with a brilliant new lighting system.

EXXON Corporation gave $1.5 million to the *American Issues Forum* and $200,000 to the National Music Council to support the *Bicentennial Parade of American Music* at the Kennedy Center in the nation's capital.

Eastman Kodak spent $1 million to build a national visitors reception center near the Washington Monument in the District of Columbia, and Sears, Roebuck and Co. donated $96,000 to the American Host Foundation for its Meet the Americans program to encourage American families to entertain visiting foreign families during the Bicentennial.

The "Continental Army"

On February 24, 1975, Administrator Warner convened a national conference of Bicentennial representatives. Held in the nation's capital, the conference concentrated on the scope and the objectives of the celebration and firmly established the federal role of working in close cooperation with the state Bicentennial organizations.

In his introductory remarks addressed to President Ford at the opening session, Administrator John Warner said, "Here today are representatives from each of the states of the union, the territories, the District of Columbia, and Puerto Rico; your Board, your Council, and members of the private sector. Mr. President, here is your 'Continental Army of 1976' . . . the spirit of this army equals in every way the spirit of Washington's army in 1776."

Tourism

Domestic and foreign tourism during the Bicentennial years was another ARBA interest. The ARBA worked closely with an informal advisory group called Travel Associations in the Bicentennial (TAB). Representing all elements of the tourism industry, TAB was formed at the ARBA's request to encourage and facilitate travel to and inside the United States.

The ARBA and the United States Travel Service published the *Travelers' Guide to Source Information*—a guide's guide that listed the best sources of information on accommodations and transportation.

The International Visitors Service Council (IVIS), the National Council for Community Services to International Visitors (COSERV) and Travelers' Aid Society all cooperated closely with the ARBA to provide touring information for foreign visitors.

The ARBA contracted with Discover America Travel Organizations, Inc. (DATO) to produce 25 biweekly regional listings of Bicentennial activities, 12 monthly "top 20" national event lists and a "top 200" summary covering the whole country. Through DATO, these releases reached just over 7,000 key press, radio and TV travel editors in 1976.

254

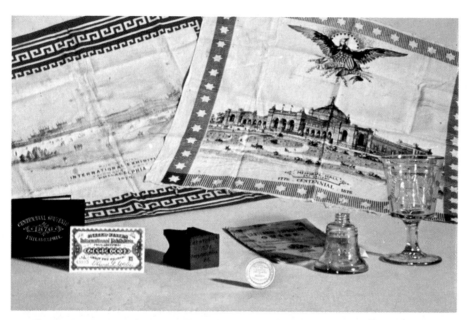

(upper left) 1876 Centennial memorabilia; (lower left) the 1976 Naticnal Bicentennial Medals; (lower right and opposite page) ARBA medals, stamps and a sample of licensed products

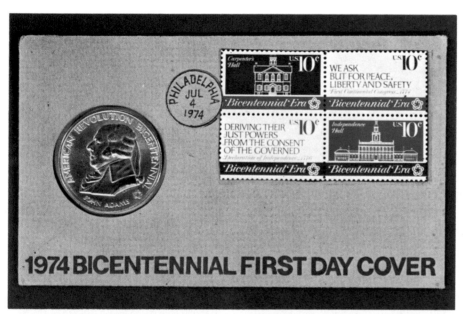

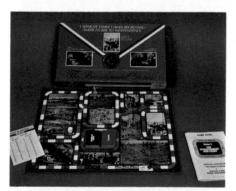

a past to remember / a future to mold

Spreading the Word

To publicize a national celebration of unprecedented scope and diversity, the ARBA employed an unusual combination of conventional and automated communications services.

Under the ARBC, development of the computerized Bicentennial Information Network (BINET) had followed the development of the national network of ARBC regional offices. By August 1973, all ARBC offices could query the central data bank of Bicentennial projects and events using ordinary telephone connections and desk-top computer terminals. BINET provided a wealth of ideas for replication by states and communities from coast to coast during the key planning year of 1974. Using the computer's ability to break projects and events out by location, subject and audience, the ARBA worked to fill gaps and eliminate overlaps in plans for Bicentennial activities.

The computer was also used to produce a series of publications which included master registers of projects and calendars of events. These hefty directories complemented the BINET computer terminal program and provided details of Bicentennial plans to the Congress, federal agencies, state commissions, all the thousands of Bicentennial communities, more than 15,000 print and broadcast media outlets, the travel and accommodations industry and the general public.

By the end of 1976, BINET had produced a series of 14 books containing 4,516 pages altogether. The nationwide distribution of 183,790 copies of these books placed over 100 million pages of Bicentennial information in the hands of those who could spread the word.

Assisting the Media

A continuing legislative requirement was to provide general information material dealing with a wide range of Bicentennial activities. The ARBC had begun that task when it periodically distributed media kits and other information aids such as public service material for TV and radio. The ARBA increased the emphasis given to public information efforts as the tempo of Bicentennial planning increased.

A Monthly Newspaper

The *Bicentennial Times* became one of the ARBA's primary general information vehicles. A tabloid published monthly, the newspaper provided information about activities, programs and events taking place in the various communities and states. It also provided information on both policy matters and Bicentennial activities in general.

Under the ARBC, circulation had grown to 65,000. The ARBA further increased the utility and the readership of the *Times.* The size of the paper grew from eight to 24 pages, and its circulation eventually reached almost 400,000. All 35 issues were distributed free of charge.

Media Used ARBA's Resources

At the same time, there was a massive effort to provide information to the media.

The ARBA's information clearinghouse of radio and television programs of historical/Bicentennial nature was widely used, and a quarterly listing of such programming was distributed to broadcast stations that wanted it. A Bicentennial network of 40 college radio stations established by the ARBA in 1975 helped stations exchange tapes of Bicentennial programming.

A four page sheet of reproductions of Bicentennial-related photographs was distributed through the National Newspaper Association in April 1976 to more than 12,000 of the country's small and medium size newspapers.

A photographic/color slide service consisting of 10,000 slides was made available to magazines, television stations, newspapers, employee publications and other audio-visual users such as exhibitors and production houses engaged in developing Bicentennial multimedia presentations.

Brochures, films and a wide variety of specialized publications were also produced. Media kits were continuously updated, and hundreds of individual news releases were circulated on a regular basis. Bumper stickers, decals and posters were likewise widely distributed.

ARBC/ARBA posters

257

Public Awareness Campaign

More steam gathered behind the ARBA's awareness program in October 1975 when a $200,000 contract was signed with Carl Byoir & Associates, Inc. a major public relations firm. In cooperation with the ARBA, the firm undertook a national campaign to support the ARBA's Bicentennial public awareness goals.

Complementing this effort, two special campaigns were aimed at reaching the Black and the Hispanic communities. The ARBA amended its contract with the Carl Byoir organization to provide $40,000 for a subcontract with B and C Associates, Inc., a Black public relations firm. The ARBA also awarded a $49,665 contract to the National Hispanic Bicentennial Commission.

Media Information Center

Capping the ARBA informational effort, a Bicentennial Weekend Media Information Center was established in Washington, D.C. in April 1976. The center was created to display and distribute information about nationwide activities planned for the weekend. It served hundreds of domestic and foreign print and broadcast journalists.

With a storehouse of information accumulated through years of careful tabulation and documentation, the center's staff was able to contribute significantly to reportage throughout the world of the dramatic, colorful and oftentimes touching celebration of America's 200th birthday.

Board and Council Actions

The ARB Board offered a firm base of support to the many ARBA decisions that had to be made.

Meeting for the first time on July 17, 1974, the Board gathered regularly

thereafter to provide policy guidance on the use of the official Bicentennial symbol, decide on policy questions relating to official recognition of national projects, set standards for the ARBA's commemorative licensing program, review and approve budgets, establish criteria for programs of matching grants-in-aid and approve grants from appropriated and nonappropriated funds.

Responding to a Board request, the President authorized the administrator to waive certain provisions of the law and limitations of authority relating to contracts and the expenditure of government funds when deemed to further the purposes of Public Law 93–179. The waivers enabled the ARBA to operate more efficiently and to make up for time lost in earlier years.

Board Approves Funds

The Board's attention was drawn to the tour program of performing groups associated with the Smithsonian Institution's 1976 *Festival of American Folklife.* The tour was threatened with cancellation when the Smithsonian ran into financial difficulty. S. Dillon Ripley,

secretary of the Institution, appealed personally to the ARBA for financial help and received several grants from nonappropriated revenues totaling $1.325 million. The Smithsonian was the largest beneficiary of ARBA funds.

The second largest beneficiary of ARBA funds was the District of Columbia. In the view of the Board, the nation's capital was to be a showcase for the Bicentennial and should provide every possible service to visitors and residents. The Board approved a total of $716,000 in special funding for the District, in addition to a total of $495,000 allotted to the District as part of the general congressionally-approved program of assistance to all state Bicentennial organizations.

The Board also approved financing totaling $75,000 in nonappropriated funds for Operation Sail '76.

Acting Administrator Jean McKee presenting Bicentennial flag to National Council of Negro Women; (opposite page) Bicentennial Ethnic/Racial Conference, Washington, D.C., June 1974.

The Magna Carta

When the British Parliament and the Queen of England agreed to loan an original copy of the Magna Carta, dated 1215, for exhibit in the Rotunda of the United States Capitol, the Board backed this unique project wholeheartedly. It approved support from nonappropriated revenues of $19,000 to prepare an illustrated brochure on the history of the document and its impact on the constitutional process in England and the United States; another $40,000 for printing a reproduction for sale in the United States Capitol and elsewhere; and $15,000 for a leaflet on the Magna Carta, to be distributed free to visitors who came to the Capitol.

Other Significant Programs

The Board also gave substantial support, in the form of matching grants, to national and international projects sponsored by nonprofit entities. In fiscal year 1975, seventy-five entities shared a total of $3,034,000. The matching funds came from the sale of ARBA medals and from the ARBA's fee from the sale of licensed articles marketed by the private sector.

Among the significant projects the Board supported were the *Citizen Involvement Network* and Boston 200, the former receiving $250,000 to help its nationwide program to set community goals, the latter $88,500 for a visitors service program which became a model for other communities across the nation.

Other representative projects included: the *Bethune Collection of Black Women's Organizations,* sponsored by the National Council of Negro Women, Inc. ($20,000); the *Navajo Zoo Park Project* of the Navajo Tribe in Window Rock, Arizona ($10,000); and the *Pacific Northwest Festival* of the Seattle Opera Association, Inc. ($25,000).

Assuring Balanced Representation

259

In addressing the criteria for approval of project grants to the states, the Board believed that there was an imbalance, that women, youth, ethnic, racial and Native American groups were not sufficiently represented in local Bicentennial projects. Accordingly, the Board stressed that ARBA grant funds should be used to assist such groups in programs that would focus on their contributions to the development of the nation—past, present and future.

Finding More Money

Congress ultimately appropriated only $11 million of the $20 million authorized in Public Law 93–179 for grants for state Bicentennial activities.

Fortunately, other sources of funds were available. In 1975, the ARBA urged state Bicentennial commissions to submit proposed Bicentennial projects for funding made available by Congress through Title X of the Public Works and Economic Development Act of 1965. This legislation authorized the Secretary of Commerce to allocate funds for the purpose of creating jobs in a period of growing unemployment. On June 24, 1975, the Department of Commerce authorized $1,833,734 for 16 Bicentennial projects around the nation that would create several thousand jobs. The ARB Board concurred with this action. A second Title X program, authorized on November 13, 1975, provided an additional $14,318,769 for an additional 99 Bicentennial projects.

The largest single group to benefit from the Title X program was the Native Americans, whose projects included amphitheaters, industries and much-needed public works. Fifty-six of their projects were funded by $6,122,700 under Title X.

ARBA Administrator John Warner and Deputy Administrator Jean McKee participate in Bicentennial programs in small towns and large cities, speaking at national conventions and biking, driving, flying, sailing and walking

Commemoratives and Licensing

Public Law 92–228 authorized a program of annual commemorative Bicentennial medals and a national medal in 1976. The ARBA enabling legislation made possible an official commemorative licensing program.

As intended by Congress, net revenues from the sale of the ARBA medals and from the ARBA licensing program provided a source of funding. The ARBA approved licenses for a variety of officially approved commemorative products. Revenues from this licensing program are estimated at a little under $1,048,000.

In the end, it was the ARBC/ARBA commemorative medal sales program that proved to be the more effective in generating revenues for funding state and local projects. The medal sales produced a net return to the ARBA of almost $21,255,000.

The medals served to increase awareness of the Bicentennial and offered an opportunity for people to collect official mementos of the nation's 200th anniversary that future generations could inherit.

Stress on Free Enterprise

Across the country, America's free enterprise and inventive genius produced an appropriately diverse range of Bicentennial commemorative products. These included items such as red, white and blue toilet seats and Bicentennial coffins. Needless to say, such items were not among those officially licensed by the ARBA, but they led to the "Buy-Centennial" criticisms of the celebration, and the ARBA became the principal target.

Thousands of different products were created, although the ARBA authorized use of the national Bicentennial symbol by only 99 licensees.

At the Economic Club in Detroit on April 26, 1976, Administrator Warner emphasized that the ARBA had no role in the marketing of the majority of these products and that it would be up to the American public to decide ultimately what was or was not in good Bicentennial taste.

Mr. Warner said that the Bicentennial, after all, was a celebration of all our freedoms—including freedom of enterprise and freedom of choice.

(top right) the National Bicentennial medals; (middle right) complete set of ARBC/ARBA solo medals in bronze and silver—1972 (no silver minted in this year), 1973, 1974, 1975, 1976; (below) July 4, 1976 fireworks at the Statue of Liberty

(opposite page) American eagle above a doorway of New England home

264 **The Cost**

The accompanying tables list gross amounts of ARBC and ARBA receipts and expenditures. Both organizations operated on small budgets, and commemorative revenues were of inestimable value in supporting thousands of Bicentennial programs.

The time lag on receipt of licensing and medal revenues produced an interesting benefit to the taxpayer. Except for $65,000 provided by a congressional appropriation, the ARBA's final year of operation—including the cost of this report—was paid for by commemorative program revenues.

For the other years, the ARBC and ARBA salaries and expenses, when apportioned among the nation's population, cost each American about 10 cents.

National Guard unit in colonial attire, Washington Monument grounds, Washington, D.C., August 1976

Funding Available to the ARBC/ARBA

(Figures in Thousands)

Fiscal Year	Congress: New Obligational Authority Appropriations	Medals and Licensing: Net Revenues	Private Sources: Donations and Misc.	Total Available Funding
1969	$ 150	—	$ 5	$ 155
1970	175	—	13	188
1971	677	—	12	689
1972	3,834 [a]	—	10	3,844
1973	6,374 [a]	$ 3,848	—	10,222
1974	19,705 [b, c]	2,322	—	22,027
1975	9,686 [c]	2,285	10	11,981
1976	11,205 [c, d]	13,138 [e]	—	24,343
1977	65	710	—	775
Totals	$51,871	$22,303 [f]	$50 [g]	$74,224

[a] Includes $2.4 million for grants to states.
[b] Includes $11 million for project grants to states.
[c] Includes $1,375,000 for operating grants to states.
[d] Covers 12 months of FY 1976 plus the three month transition quarter.
[e] Includes national medals revenue and all licensing income.
[f] Total as of December 1976; additional returns are expected.
[g] Includes cash ($13,000) and goods and services ($37,000).

Summary of Total ARBC/ARBA Grants to Bicentennial Organizations of the States, Territories, District of Columbia and the Commonwealth of Puerto Rico

Nonappropriated funds for project matching grants, $40,000 per entity:	
FY 1974*	$ 2,150,000
FY 1975	2,200,000
FY 1976	2,200,000
Calendar 1976	2,200,000
Appropriated funds for administrative assistance grants:	
FY 1972 (states—$45,000; territories—$30,000)	2,400,000
FY 1973—Same	2,400,000
FY 1974 ($25,000 to both states and territories)	1,375,000
FY 1975—Same	1,375,000
FY 1976—Same	1,375,000
Appropriated funds for project matching grants, $200,000 to each state and territory (FY 1974–75):	11,000,000
Public Works and Economic Development Act Title X funds, earmarked for Bicentennial project-related jobs:	
Phase I	1,833,734
Phase II	14,318,769
Total	$44,827,503

*Approved in FY 1973; obligated in FY 1974. Entities other than states received $30,000 each in this fiscal year.

Use of Funds by the ARBC/ARBA, FY 1969—FY 1977

	Amount	Percent
Matching States Project Grants	$19,750,000	26.7
General Administration	19,164,000*	25.8
Direct States Assistance Grants	8,925,000	12.0
Program Development	7,425,000	10.0
National/International Program Funding	7,200,000	9.7
Exhibits and Films	4,305,000	5.8
Regional Offices	4,100,000	5.5
Master Calendar	2,385,000	3.2
Returned to U.S. Treasury	970,000	1.3
TOTAL	$74,224,000*	100.0

*Includes $50,000 consisting of donations of goods and services ($37,000) and cash ($13,000)

Epilogue

During a troubled period of our short history, the Bicentennial parted a curtain. Behind it we saw an America that still firmly believes in the principles of its founders.

The outpouring of national spirit and pride which marked the 1976 Fourth of July weekend was without precedent.

Some had lamented the absence of a traditional centerpiece for the celebration, such as a world's fair or the Olympics.

We discovered that a centerpiece had been there all along. It was America and its people. From the imposing Operation Sail '76 in New York Harbor to the dramatic last encampment of the *Bicentennial Wagon Train Pilgrimage to Pennsylvania* at Valley Forge, Pennsylvania after its trek eastward and the thousands of parades, parties, fireworks displays and religious services everywhere, the nation had turned a festive red, white and blue.

The accomplishments of America's Bicentennial celebration may never be fully acknowledged during the lifetimes of those who worked so hard to produce them. Yet there is food for thought for those scholars of the future who may look back and bring those accomplishments into bolder relief than they are now.

Almost Everybody Joined In

Measured only in terms of the number of Bicentennial Communities registered and recognized by the American Revolution Bicentennial Commission (ARBC) and American Revolution Bicentennial Administration (ARBA), the celebration unquestionably inspired the largest popular participation in a national observance in our history.

The ARBC/ARBA *Bicentennial Communities Program* was surely the spark that gave the celebration its widely acknowledged grassroots character, involving or affecting as it did some 90 percent of the population of the United States.

At international, national, regional, state and local levels, the Bicentennial produced unprecedented digging into the country's origins and history.

Vote!—Alameda's Challenge

Some states and hundreds of communities made voter registration one of their major Bicentennial objectives, since 1976, like 1876, was the year of a presidential election.

The city of Alameda, California, for example, issued a challenge in the summer of 1975 to all other communities, large and small, to vie with it for the title of "votingest city." The challenge was eventually picked up by more than 200 municipalities. The ARBA itself provided funds to spearhead a voter registration and "get out the vote" drive in the fall of 1976 as one of its final contributions to the Bicentennial. The Advertising Council, Inc. joined in the effort.

Our Cultural Diversity

The Bicentennial emphasis on the nation's cultural diversity was surely one of the Bicentennial's hallmarks. Focusing as it did on the longstanding tradition of "hyphenated Americanism," the Bicentennial provided the nation's ethnic and racial groups with a major opportunity to show pride in their contributions to the growth of America.

There were continuing recriminations about the past, and all old wounds certainly were not healed in 1976. But public attention to the accomplishments of ethnic and racial groups, and in particular those of Blacks and Native Americans, was a Bicentennial achievement of large dimension.

Celebrate the July 4th feeling on November 2nd.

Vote. It's the Bicentennial thing to do.

"Our Celebration Has Done Much . . ."

When President Gerald R. Ford accepted Administrator Warner's resignation as head of the ARBA on September 30, 1976, he wrote: "Our celebration of the 200th anniversary of our independence has done much to reinforce the confidence, pride and vitality of the American people. Under your steady hand, ARBA has been instrumental in helping us strengthen our links with the events and traditions that have made us the great Nation we are while at the same time opening the way to the promise and challenge of our third century."

Only a handful of the 230 people who worked for the ARBA at the height of the celebrations were on hand to write this report, as directed by the Congress, and to fold the ARBA tent on June 30, 1977. The few remaining functions were handed over to the Department of the Interior.

If the Bicentennial celebration had proved nothing else, it had proved, in the words of John Warner, that "America was alive and well in 1976."

(opposite page, top) Get out the vote campaign for 1976; (bottom) Advertising Council, Inc. national public service vote campaign

Acknowledgements

Photo Credits, Volumes I–V

ARBA Staff Photographer:

Fred Figall, Washington, D.C.

ARBA Contract Photographers:

Ross V. Chapple, Washington, D.C.
Paul Conklin, Washington, D.C.
Fletcher Drake, Washington, D.C.
Warren Goldberg, Boston, MA
Patricia Herrewig, Washington, D.C.
John Neubauer, Washington, D.C.
Tommy Noonan, Purcellville, VA
W. W. Parish, Washington, D.C.
Charles H. Phillips, Laurel, MD
Jack Silver, Washington, D.C.

Contributing Photographers:

Allied Pix Services, Inc.,
    Harrisburg, PA
Ankers Capitol Photographers,
    Washington, D.C.
JO1 Atchison, U.S. Navy
Ted Austin, Washington, D.C.
Jim Aycock, Washington, D.C.
Jonathan Barkan, Somerville, MA
Barlow Photography, St. Louis, MO
Herbert Barnes, Williamsburg, VA
John Barrett, Helena, MT
Linda Biznez, Sacramento, CA
Neal Boenzi, *The New York Times,*
    New York, NY
Walter J. Booze, Washington, D.C.
Richard Braaten, John F. Kennedy
    Center for the Performing Arts,
    Washington, D.C.
Brooks Photographers, Bethesda, MD
Morris T. Brown, II, Wilmington, DE
Harry L. Burnett, Jr., Washington, D.C.
Bill Butler, Vienna, VA
Kelly Bryant, Little Rock, AR
Benito Don Cabrera, Washington, D.C.
Harold Caldwell, Fargo, ND
Clinton A. Chaney, Boise, ID
Kee T. Chang, Chicago, IL
Arch Cheney, Jr., Salt Lake City, UT

Jorden Davie, Little Rock, AR
Richard Dean, Tucson, AZ
Gabriel R. Delobbe, Ft. Wayne, IN
Dome City Photographers, Inc.,
    Houston, TX
Dorf Photography, Austin, TX
Dufor Photographers, Philadelphia, PA
BM1 R. R. Egan, U.S. Navy
David Falconer, Black Star,
    New York, NY
Herbert C. Force, Niagara Falls, NY
P. Formato, Hartford, CT
Richard Frear, Washington, D.C.
Nick Freda, Bowie, MD
Sy Friedman, New York, NY
Gaines Studio, Kennesaw, GA
Peter Galindo, Sioux Falls, SD
Doug Gamage, Riverside, RI
Richard Gardner, Memphis, TN
Garrett Photography, Boise, ID
Robert C. Gibbs, Marshall, MO
W. J. Gire, Tacoma, WA
Alan N. Gold, Passaic, NJ
Pat Hall, Cheyenne, WY
G. N. Hancock, Clarendon, TX
Frank Harrington, Kansas City, MO
Karl Holland, Tallahassee, FL
John Hopf, Newport, RI
Duane Howell, *Denver Post,* Denver, CO
Alyce Jackson, Washington, D.C.
Joennes Studio, Boonville, MO
Bob Jones, USCG, Honolulu, HI
Susanne King, Hartford, CT
Guy Kramer, Seattle, WA
Joseph Kugielsky, Westport, CT
SP5 Paul Lambert, Military District of
    Washington, D.C.
John A. Leone Photographers,
    Trenton, NJ
Lopez-Medina, Quincy, IL
Marler Photography, Alexandria, VA
Fred J. Maroon, Washington, D.C.
Fred W. Marvel, Oklahoma City, OK
Jean McKee, Washington, D.C.
Robert H. McNeill, Washington, D.C.
Dan Milburn, Phoenix, AZ

PH2 Terry Mitchell, U.S. Navy
CJO Richard Montgomery, U.S. Navy
D. Morton, San Francisco, CA
Bob Murphy, Chicago, IL
Paul Myatt, Washington, D.C.
Tom Myers, Beaver, PA
Vardell C. Nesbitt, Washington, D.C.
Norton Pearl Photography,
    Burlingame, CA
Dick Oakland, Washington, D.C.
Dexter Oliver, Washington, D.C.
PH1 N. K. Palosky, U.S. Navy
H. Parson, Hoboken/Antwerp, Belgium
Paul Patton, Oklahoma
Rip Payne Photos, Charlottesville, VA
Roy Perry, Montgomery County, MD
Photo Ideas, Inc., Chicago, IL
Pictures, Inc., Boston, MA
Ivan Pintar, Scottsdale, AZ
André Proulx, Canada
Arlen R. Ramsay, Southfield, MI
Reed and Susan Erskine,
    Washington, D.C.
Lawrence S. Reynolds, Los Angeles, CA
Mike Riley, La Grange, GA
Ed Roseberry, Charlottesville, VA
Jack Rottier, Washington, D.C.
Tom Salyer, Spokane, WA
Flip Schulke, Black Star, New York, NY
George W. Self, San Diego, CA
Jens Selvig, Ad-Art Productions,
    Billings, MT
Larry Shirkey, Denver, CO
Dennis R. Smith, Clinton, MD
Peggy M. Smith, Clinton, MD
L. Storsater, Canadian Embassy,
    Washington, D.C.
Tradelinks Photo, Ernakulam,
    Kerala, India
Vanguard Photography,
    San Francisco, CA
Vano Photography, San Francisco, CA
Lissa Vogt, Silver Spring, MD
Voscar Studio, Presque Isle, ME
Dick Wartinger, Miamisburg, OH
PH2 Timothy A. Wehr, U.S. Navy

Fred Weicht, Wilmington, DE
Mrs. M. Weinstein, Forest Hills, NY
Keith Weller, Ellicott City, MD
Jesse Wallace West, Centre, AL
C. Westerman, Louisville, KY
Kent Williams, San Francisco, CA
Thomas L. Williams, Williamsburg, VA
Dave Wilson, U.S. Navy
Marilyn Wilson, Future Homemakers of
    America, Kenai Peninsula, AK
Don E. Wolter, Kenwood, CA
Wondrasek Photography, Bottineau, ND
Zodiac Photographers, New York, NY

270 **Bicentennial Organizations of the 50 States, Commonwealth of Puerto Rico, District of Columbia and Territories of American Samoa, Guam and the Virgin Islands, and the Following**

Alameda Vote '76; Alexandria Bicentennial Commission

Baton Rouge Bicentennial Commission; Bicentennial Horizons of American Music; Bikecentennial '76; Boston 200; Bowling Green State University; Broward Community College

Colonial Williamsburg; Committee for the Future

De Anza College; De Anza Expedition Committee; Detroit Bicentennial Commission; Dominguez-Escalante State-Federal Bicentennial Committee

The Forest County Potawatomie Community, Inc.

Galveston County Bicentennial Committee; Goessel Bicentennial Committee

Village of Hamburg; Hampton American Revolution Bicentennial Celebration Committee; Howell Bicentennial Committee

Idaho Department of Parks and Recreation

Kansas Department of Transportation

Lexington Bicentennial Committee

Maryland Department of Economic and Community Development; Mitchell County Bicentennial; Montgomery County Bicentennial Commission

Nevada State Museum; Niagara Falls Bicentennial Committee; North Carolina State Department of Archives and History

Ohio Historical Society; Ohio University School of Theater; "Old Fashioned Days '75"; OPSAIL '76

The Pittsburg Bicentennial-Centennial, Inc.; Pocatello-Bannock Bicentennial Commission

Ripon College; Rocky Boy Elementary School

St. Francis Bicentennial Committee; San Antonio Bicentennial Committee; Shreveport Bicentennial Commission

Third Century U.S.A.

Vermont Department of Highways

Westport, Connecticut American Revolution Bicentennial Committee; University of Wyoming

Yakima American Revolution Bicentennial Commission; York County Bicentennial Commission

Associations, Businesses, Media and Organizations

ABC–TV; The Advertising Council, Inc.; The Aitkin-Kynett Co., Inc.; Albion American Heritage Publishing Co., AMERICANA

Beaver County Times; Bedford, Indiana Chamber of Commerce

Camden County Public Relations; CBS–TV; Centennial Cakes; *Centralia Sentinel;* Century Publications, Inc.; Chesebrough-Pond's Inc.; Communications Unlimited; Countryman-Klang, Inc.; *The Courier-Journal* and *The Louisville Times*

Deseret News; The Detroit News; Dudley-Anderson-Yutzy

Edward Gottlieb & Associates; Eli Productions

Future Homemakers of America

Haycox Productions; The Henry Ford Museum; *The Honolulu Advertiser*

International Business Machines Corporation (IBM)

J. C. Penney Co., Inc.; J. W. B. Enterprises, Inc.; Jennings Publications; Jerre R. Todd & Associates

Kennebec Journal; Kitchens of Sarah Lee; Krementz & Co.

Las Vegas News Bureau

Mackinas Bridge Authority; Mekler/Ansell Associates, Inc.; *The Minneapolis Tribune*

National Guard Association; NBC–TV; New York Racing Association

The Pillowry; Pilot Club; Porter Novelli & Associates, Inc.; Prudential Center

Ogden Reporter; Richmond Newspaper, Inc.; Rhode Island Historical Society; Rockefeller Center, Inc.; Ruder & Finn, Inc.

City of Seattle, Department of Parks & Recreation; Setter & Associates, Inc.; Sister Cities, International

Today Show, NBC–TV

University of Arizona Alumni Association

Virgin Islands Telephone Corporation

Walt Disney Productions; Washington Cathedral; *Washington Star News*

Yucaipa & Calimesa News-Mirror

Federal Government Departments and Agencies

The White House; The House of Representatives

Department of Agriculture; U.S. Air Force; Architect of the Capitol; U.S. Army; Army, Fort Myer, VA; U.S. Army Corps of Engineers; Army Photographic Branch, Ft. Benning, GA

U.S. Coast Guard

U.S. Government Printing Office

Department of Health, Education, and Welfare

Department of the Interior

John F. Kennedy Center for the Performing Arts

Library of Congress

U.S. Mint

National Aeronautics and Space Administration; National Archives and Records Service; National Park Service; U.S. Navy Photographic Center

Smithsonian Institution

Wright-Patterson Air Force Base, OH

Foreign Governments and Organizations

Canadian Embassy, Washington, D.C.; County Tyrone, Northern Ireland

Danish Information Office, Consulate General of Denmark, Washington, D.C.

German Information Center, New York, NY

Ministère de l'Information, Niamey, Niger

American Revolution Bicentennial Administration

2401 E Street, N.W.
Washington, D.C. 20276

This report has been written, printed and distributed in accordance with Sections 7(b) and 10(i) of Public Law 93–179, dated December 11, 1973.

U.S. Senator Edward W. Brooke
Chairman, ARB Board

Dr. J. Duane Squires
Vice-chairman, ARB Board

David L. Wolper
Chairman, ARB Advisory Council

Ann Hawkes Hutton
Vice-chairwoman, ARB Advisory Council

Jean McKee
ARBA Acting Administrator

Staff

271

Editorial Board: William L. Blue, Hugh A. Hall, Herbert E. Hetu, Jean McKee, Eugene J. Skora

Editors: Daniel S. Buser, Jr., Herbert E. Hetu, Edward K. Zimmerman

Associate Editors: Virginia D. Armstrong, Catherine E. Farrell, Mark Guidry, Daniel D. McKenzie, John S. Scholzen

Style Editor: H. Whitney Watriss

Contributing Editors: Nancy L. Blair, Paul F. Brewster, William P. Butler, Cherrie H. Hall, Julian K. Morrison, III, Nicholas Ruggieri

Photographic Editors: Daniel S. Buser, Jr., Catherine E. Farrell

Researchers: Oralia V. Aldrete, Ruth A. Bosek, Jean E. Boyer, Stephen G. Goodrich, Elizabeth J. Kirby, Peggy M. Smith

Editorial Support Staff: Janet K. Anderson, Kathleen Biondolillo, Patricia L. Braxton, Carol J. Byers, Linda T. Cole, Jerome B. Coll, Sherry F. Cross, Charles F. Goodspeed, Erla M. Kratzer, Gregory A. Manero, James W. Mansfield, Priscilla H. Penn, Anita L. Roby, Margaret A. Schrader, Peggy M. Smith, Maura A. Vaughan, Monica Vaughan, Arnold C. Williams, Hazel R. Wyman

Distribution: Richard N. Bain, Joyce E. Tobin

Design: Nicholas M. Freda, U.S. Government Printing Office

Typographic Coordinator: William W. Chenoweth, U.S. Government Printing Office

Printing Coordinator: Donald E. Sullivan, Department of the Interior

Index

275

These volumes were printed on an offset press.

Text type for volumes I, II and the preliminary pages and opening spreads for the chapters in volumes III, IV and V is 9/11 Helvetica. Main heads are 18 point Helvetica, subheads are 9 point Helvetica bold and photo captions are 9/11 Helvetica italic. The listing of state events in volumes III, IV and V is 7/7 Spartan Book Condensed, medium and heavy. All type was produced by high speed photocomposition.

Text paper for volumes I and II is 70 pound white litho-coated offset paper; paper for volumes III, IV and V is 60 pound white offset book paper.

The covers and slip case are white pyroxylin impregnated book cloth with an overcoat of rub-resistant clear varnish.

All binding is by the Smythe sewn method.

☆ U.S. Government Printing Office : 1977 O—222-656